**Issues in
Labor Policy**

Issues in Labor Policy

Papers in Honor of
Douglass Vincent Brown

Edited by
Stanley M. Jacks

The MIT Press, Cambridge, Massachusetts, and London, England

Set in Linotype Baskerville by The Book Press
Printed and bound in the United States of America by The Book Press

ISBN 0 262 10 009 6 (hardcover)

Library of Congress catalog card number: 73–148965

Foreword

Douglass Brown has had such a wide influence on the quality of scholarship and performance in the field of labor and industrial relations that it would be difficult to overstate it, for it is an influence that is largely expressed in the work of his students and his colleagues. It often happens that great teaching is not recognized and appreciated for its full worth, but happily this has not been the case with Professor Brown.

Generations of M.I.T. students, undergraduate, graduate, and postgraduate, will remember many personal instances in which he counseled, prodded, pressed, or queried—all in the interest of the educational process of making it possible for his students to become what they truly were. Neither his time nor his patience had limits when it came to helping his students and his colleagues. Now we salute him and give him this expression of thanks, affection, and respect.

Howard W. Johnson
President,
Massachusetts Institute of Technology

This volume to honor Douglass Brown is most appropriate, and I welcome this opportunity to say a word about him.

His influence on me, as on so many others, has been and is a great and good one. His "students" are legion and include all manner of associates at M.I.T. and outside the institution's formal boundaries, as well as the students of his students of his students. When people speak of the multiplier effect of a great teacher, they must have Douglass Brown in mind and in view.

Two aspects of Professor Brown's character and pattern of behavior are especially noteworthy just now.

He has great respect for the individual person. This begins with self-respect and continues to an acceptance of honestly held differences in views. He will argue but never try to force his views on anyone else.

He is the same man—over time, in different places, and among different people. He is himself. Long before the idea was discovered by the current young generation, Douglass Brown had been doing his own thing. And a wonderful thing it is.

George P. Shultz
Director, Office of Management and Budget,
formerly Secretary of Labor

Douglass Brown is honored in this volume by students and colleagues who recognize him to be M.I.T.'s most influential teacher in industrial relations. I have worked with him in the M.I.T. Industrial Relations Section for thirty years, in a close professional association that extends over a longer period than most in our field. From this long experience I can say with feeling that as a colleague, coauthor, and counselor he has no equal.

It is fitting that, last year, his profession should honor Douglass Brown by electing him president of the Industrial Relations Research Association. This high honor is the culmination of a notable list of professional distinctions, including his long and influential service as a member of the Research Advisory Board of the Committee for Economic

Development and his charter membership in the National Academy of Arbitrators.

We at M.I.T. are especially pleased that Professor Brown will continue to teach part time. He has often said that courses are really about the people who give them. We wish there could be no term at M.I.T. when you could not take a course about Douglass Brown.

Charles A. Myers
Sloan Fellows Professor of Management
and Director, Industrial Relations Section,
Massachusetts Institute of Technology

Contributors

Solomon B. Levine	Professor of Economics and Business, University of Wisconsin
J. W. Miller, Jr.	Vice-President, Personnel and Organization, B. F. Goodrich Company
Charles A. Myers	Sloan Fellows Professor of Management and Director, Industrial Relations Section, Massachusetts Institute of Technology
Michael J. Piore	Associate Professor of Economics, Massachusetts Institute of Technology
George P. Shultz	Director, Office of Management and Budget, formerly Secretary of Labor
George Strauss	Professor of Business Administration, University of California, Berkeley
David P. Taylor	Executive Assistant to the Director, Office of Management and Budget, formerly Associate Professor of Industrial Relations, Massachusetts Institute of Technology
John G. Turnbull	Associate Dean, College of Liberal Arts, University of Minnesota

Publications and Papers of Douglass Vincent Brown January 1970

"New South Wales Family Endowment Act, 1927." *Quarterly Journal of Economics* 42 (May 1928).

"Family Allowances." Ph.D. thesis. Harvard University, 1932.

[with Edward Chamberlain, Seymour E. Harris, et al.] *Economics of the Recovery Program.* New York: McGraw-Hill, 1934.

[with M. M. Moore] "The Cost of Institutional Care of Epileptics in Massachusetts." *New England Journal of Medicine* 219 (July 21, 1938).

[with John T. Dunlop, Edwin M. Martin, Charles A. Myers, and John A. Brownell] *Industrial Wage Rates, Labor Costs, and Price Policies.* Temporary National Economic Committee Monograph no. 5. 76th Cong., 3rd sess. Washington, D.C.: Government Printing Office, 1940.

"Should Unions Be Made 'Responsible'?" *Mechanical Engineering* 66 (January 1944). (Review of Joel Seidman's *Union Rights and Union Duties* [New York: Harcourt, Brace, 1943].)

"Review of Experiences in Connection with Labor Contracts and Arbitration." Paper presented at the Labor-Management Relations Conference, sponsored by Barnes Textile Associates. Boston, June 7–8, 1944.

"Economic Factors Influencing Labor Relations in the Forthcoming Year." Executive Seminar Series on Industrial Relations, 1946–1947, Session 1, University of Chicago, Industrial Relations Center, 1946.

"Mediation Works." (A brief examination of mediation as an aid in collective bargaining.) *CED Digest* 1 (April 1947).

"Management Rights and the Collective Agreement." *Proceedings of the First Annual Meeting,* Industrial Relations Research Association, December 1948.

"Management Rights—What Changes Are Occurring?" *Report of the First Industrial Relations Conference.* Montreal: University of Montreal Industrial Relations Section, 1949.

[Comment on] "Framework for the Analysis of Industrial Relations." *Industrial and Labor Relations Review* 3 (April 1950).

"Labor and Antitrust Laws." *Proceedings of the American Bar Association, Section on Labor Relations Law,* 1955.

[with Charles A. Myers] "The Changing Industrial Relations Philosophy of American Management." *Proceedings of the Ninth Annual Meeting,* Industrial Relations Research Association, December 1956.

"The Impact of Some NLRB Decisions." *Proceedings of the Thirteenth Annual Meeting,* Industrial Relations Research Association, December 1960.

[with George P. Shultz] "Public Policy and the Structure of Collective Bargaining." In *The Structure of Collective Bargaining*. Edited by A. R. Weber. New York: Free Press of Glencoe, 1961.

"Management Problems." Paper read at the Sixth Annual Industrial Relations Conference (Problems of Changing Power Relationships in Collective Bargaining), University of Michigan–Wayne State University Institute of Labor and Industrial Relations, Ann Arbor, 1961.

The Public Interest in National Labor Policy. New York: Committee for Economic Development, 1961. (Member of the Independent Study Group.)

[with Charles A. Myers] "Historical Evolution." In *Public Policy and Collective Bargaining*. Edited by J. Shister, B. Aaron, and C. W. Summers. New York: Harper & Row, 1962.

"An Appraisal of Profit Sharing." *Management Record* (National Industrial Conference Board) 24 (December 1962).

Introduction

This volume contains seven papers written in honor of Douglass V. Brown on the occasion of his retirement from the faculty of the Massachusetts Institute of Technology in June 1969. The papers were first presented at a symposium on May 1, 1969, attended by friends of Professor Brown.

Each of the authors has taught in the Institute's Industrial Relations Section, and five of them—Levine, Miller, Shultz, Strauss, and Turnbull—took their doctorates at M.I.T. Their contributions to this volume express for a generation of students of industrial relations some measure of the profound respect and abiding friendship they bear for Professor Brown. For them, he has been *the* teacher, the man who has set the moral and intellectual standard to which they have aspired.

Douglass Brown's tenure coincides with the emergence of a national labor policy. He received his doctoral degree at Harvard in 1932, three years before the Wagner Act. He came to M.I.T. in 1938 when the fate of collective bargaining policy was still unclear. The unfolding story of labor relations policy over thirty years has been his central interest, and his perceptive and daring critique of policy issues has enlightened the deliberations of the Committee for Economic Development, the Industrial Relations Research Association, and the National Academy of Arbitrators, as well as the councils of government. But it has been in the classroom that the focus of his intellectual and moral power has been most brilliant. Skeptical of the popular view on any matter and disdainful of prepackaged ideas, he has pressed upon his students the intractable facts and hard choices that the real world presents. This he has done with such grace and humor that all who have passed his way know that softness of spirit need not be sacrificed for toughness of mind.

Professor Brown began his teaching career at Harvard, where he tutored in economics and later served as assistant professor of medical economics at the Harvard Medical School. He was a professor of industrial relations at the Massachusetts Institute of Technology until 1946, when he became the first Alfred P. Sloan Professor of Management.

Although the committee that organized the honorary symposium for Professor Brown gave no thought to setting a theme for the papers, four of them (Myers, Piore and Taylor, Shultz, and Strauss) deal with aspects of manpower policy. Two papers (Levine and Miller) evaluate collective bargaining as a national policy—one dealing with American experience and the other with postwar policy in Japan. The seventh paper (Turnbull) traces the evolution of the field of labor studies over the last three decades, the period of Douglass Brown's tenure at M.I.T.

Professor Charles A. Myers and Dean Abraham J. Siegel of the Sloan School assisted the editor in the arrangements for the symposium. The invaluable help of Patte Macpherson and Sue Brooker should also be acknowledged. Jean Barrett typed much of the manuscript.

Stanley M. Jacks
Senior Lecturer,
Sloan School of Management

Cambridge, Massachusetts
December 1970

Issues in Labor Policy

1

Critical Issues in National Manpower Policy

Charles A. Myers

The Nixon administration has already modified as well as built on the manpower policies and programs developed under the Johnson and Kennedy administrations.[1] While a great deal of manpower training and development occurs within enterprises and organizations, the federal government cannot escape the responsibility for guiding and funding programs to aid those without work who have been termed "disadvantaged," as well as certain groups among the 77 million who have jobs. Federal support and business initiative have in fact combined in the JOBS (Job Opportunities in the Business Sector) program of the National Alliance of Businessmen.

The federal initiative did not start with the Kennedy administration. The Employment Act of 1946 committed the nation to achieve and maintain a high level of employment. Since then, it has been widely recognized that without a high level of effective demand and the maintenance of a low rate of unemployment (less than 4 percent), those who have been trained will not find jobs.[2] Thus we need both

[1] Since this paper was written before the reorganization of the present Manpower Administration in the Department of Labor and the introduction of new legislation, it does not cover these developments in detail. I am indebted to Garth L. Mangum and Sar A. Levitan for comments on a preliminary draft, completed early in 1969.

[2] The Joint Economic Committee of the Congress has pointed out: "A rise of one percentage point in the overall unemployment rate would involve approximately three-quarters of a million people—a magnitude which dwarfs present manpower programs and is perhaps larger than all of the manpower training and employment programs put together. Indeed, the programs designed to encourage employment and training in the private sector will surely fail if there is a significant weakening

high demand and improvement of the supply (quality) of people seeking jobs. The drop in the unemployment rate between the third quarter of 1967 and the third quarter of 1968 in the poor neighborhoods of the nation's 100 largest cities from 6.6 percent to 5.9 percent (still higher than the national average) was accounted for almost entirely by the drop in nonwhite unemployment relative to white unemployment.[3] While nonwhite unemployment was still higher than white unemployment in urban poverty areas, white unemployment continued at 5.2 percent. With the efforts of the present administration to reduce inflationary pressures, unemployment in these areas will certainly increase again.

Other federal programs tried to bring jobs to where people lived, such as the Area Redevelopment Act and the subsequent Economic Development Act. In 1962 Congress passed the Manpower Development and Training Act, followed by the Economic Opportunity Act (the so-called "poverty program"), and in September 1968 the new Vocational Education Act (which expanded the earlier 1963 act).

We are approaching the components, if not the scale, of a national manpower policy, but there are still many unresolved issues. In this paper, I have chosen to consider

---

in the aggregate demand." U.S. Congress, Report of the Joint Economic Committee, *Employment and Manpower Problems in the Cities: Implications of the National Advisory Commission on Civil Disorders,* 90th Cong., 2nd sess. (1968), p. 4.

[3] Data from the U.S. Bureau of Labor Statistics, reported in Bureau of National Affairs, *Daily Labor Report,* October 23, 1968. Despite this progress, it should be noted that on a comparative basis unemployment rates in the United States have consistently been higher than those of Sweden, West Germany, and Japan, for example.

seven that seem to me of primary importance.[4] Others might be included and would be given different emphasis by manpower specialists. Many of the seven listed here have been discussed elsewhere,[5] and the new manpower programs of the present administration purport to deal with a large number of them. The seven issues to be considered are:

1. Inadequate funding of manpower programs.
2. Lack of effective coordination at the federal level.
3. Consequent weaknesses in the "delivery system" at the state and local levels.
4. The problem of "community control" of manpower programs, particularly in urban areas.
5. Federal financing of private training and job-development efforts, including the issues of subsidies versus tax incentives.
6. Guaranteed employment versus guaranteed income (as exemplified by the negative income tax and family allowance proposals).

[4] Many of the ideas developed in this paper have grown out of my membership on the National Manpower Policy Task Force, a private nonprofit organization for studies and research in manpower policy, with headquarters in Washington, D.C. A consensus of the views of the Task Force was presented in a position paper, *The Nation's Manpower Programs* (Washington, D.C., 1969).

[5] See the University of Michigan–Wayne State University Institute of Labor and Industrial Relations, Policy Papers in Human Resources and Industrial Relations, especially no. 2, Sar A. Levitan and Garth L. Mangum, *Making Sense of Federal Manpower Policy* (Ann Arbor, 1967); no. 5, Garth L. Mangum, *Contributions and Costs of Manpower Development and Training* (Ann Arbor, 1967); and no. 6, Charles C. Killingsworth, *Jobs and Income for Negroes* (Ann Arbor, 1968). All three were published jointly with the National Manpower Policy Task Force.

7. Interrelationships of manpower programs and other programs dealing with the urban crisis.

It is important to reemphasize the progress that has been made in developing adequate manpower policies under federal initiative during the seven years since the passage of the Manpower Development and Training Act (MDTA) in 1962. There have been shortcomings, and these will be pointed out, but we have also learned a great deal about which programs are most effective, how they can be delivered, and how a partnership between government and the private sector can be developed. Critics of our manpower policies neglect the fact that our system of public education, which has developed over a much longer period, is far from perfect. Indeed, it is the deficiencies of secondary education (including vocational education) that have led to school dropouts and poorly prepared job applicants in many cities. The failings in our school system have required the remedial education and training programs that recent manpower policies have tried to provide. While there is still much to be done to avoid shortages of high-talent manpower, the education and training of professionals and subprofessionals have probably received more attention in our educational system than the needs of those at the bottom of the occupational ladder or of those who have never had employment.

Inadequate Funding of Manpower Programs

Funds for federally supported manpower programs in 1968 (fiscal year ending June 30) totaled about $2.2 billion. This figure includes not only the programs under the Manpower

Development and Training Act ($416 million) but also other programs funded under the Department of Labor, such as the U.S. Employment Service and the Bureau of Apprenticeship and Training (both now part of the Manpower Administration in the Department), which added $311 million. In addition, Vocational Education, Vocational Rehabilitation, and Adult Basic Education were funded under the Department of Health, Education, and Welfare, for a total of $822 million in fiscal 1968. Finally, the Office of Economic Opportunity funded such programs as Neighborhood Youth Corps, Job Corps, Work Experience and Training (for relief recipients and other needy persons), Operation Mainstream, New Careers, Special Impact, and the manpower efforts of Community Action Programs—all for a total of $733 million. Some of these OEO programs were administered by the Manpower Administration of the Department of Labor.[6]

The 1968 total of about $2.2 billion represents a steady increase from $245 million in 1961 (before the MDTA was passed) and $1.377 billion in 1965, when the poverty program got under way. First-time enrollments in manpower

[6] Data from Sar A. Levitan and Garth L. Mangum, *Federal Work and Training Programs in the 1960's* (Detroit: Wayne State University Press, 1969). For another tabulation that includes *all* education and military training, see *Special Analyses, Budget of the United States, Fiscal Year 1969* (Washington, D.C.: Government Printing Office, 1968), Table H–1, Federal Funds for Education, Training and Related Programs by Level or Type, p. 97. The total amount involved in these programs, including manpower programs summarized in the text above, is $10.7 billion, of which $6.7 billion is for education (excluding vocational) and $1.6 billion for military training. The fiscal 1969 manpower budget in the Department of Labor is $2.4 billion, or slightly higher than the fiscal 1968 figure for the same programs.

programs rose from 12,000 in 1962 to 1,300,000 in fiscal 1968.[7]

Present funding for manpower programs needs to be evaluated in relation to existing needs and the effectiveness of the programs now in operation. The latter is more difficult, for cost-benefit analyses of manpower programs, like other public programs, involve assumptions about experimental and control groups, length of the period, whether other factors remain the same, and so on.[8] Nevertheless, the limited evidence we have indicates that certain types of programs have been successful but need more funds. These include (1) MDT—institutional training through skill centers and other training facilities; (2) the supporting services, such as counseling, special remedial education, and medical services, which are needed to deal with the problems facing the disadvantaged as they prepare for employment; and (3) the in-school Neighborhood Youth Corps, which provides up to fifteen hours of after-school employment to encourage youth from poor homes to remain in school, plus

[7] *Manpower Report of the President* (Washington, D.C.: Government Printing Office, 1969), Table 14, p. 140.

[8] For a discussion of evaluation studies, see Garth L. Mangum, *MDTA: Foundation of Federal Manpower Policy* (Baltimore: Johns Hopkins Press, 1968), Chapter 4, and D. Quinn Mills, "The Evaluation of Manpower Training Programs," paper prepared for the U.S. Department of Commerce, Economic Development Administration Research Conference, Washington, D.C., February 1968. See also Worth Bateman, "An Application of Cost-Benefit Analysis to the Work-Experience Program," *Papers and Proceedings of the American Economic Association* 58 (May 1968): 80–90, and Gerald G. Somers, "Data Needs for Monitoring and Evaluating Manpower Programs," *Proceedings of the Twenty-first Annual Meeting,* Industrial Relations Research Association, December 1968.

summer employment.[9] While estimates are crude, up to $1 billion more could be used to meet existing needs, including expansion of present on-the-job training programs with federal subsidies.[10]

The needs are clear. Unpublished data prepared by the Manpower Administration of the U.S. Department of Labor late in 1968 showed the following numbers of people in disadvantaged groups, estimated for 1969 as the "universe of need":

Note that this rough total is far beyond the half-million

Unemployed (long-term, or 15 weeks or more, plus short-term unemployed poor)	1,000,000
Part-time for economic reasons	1,720,000
Out of the labor force but should be employed	4,300,000
Employed full time year-round, but at poverty-level wages	5,950,000
	12,970,000[11]

9 These conclusions have emerged from discussions at meetings of the National Manpower Policy Task Force. For data on first-time enrollments in all federally assisted manpower programs 1962–1968, see *Manpower Report of the President,* Table 14, p. 140.

10 The present administration has indicated that subsidized on-the-job training programs will be expanded, but the Job Corps (transferred entirely to the Department of Labor early in 1969) has been substantially curtailed at a saving of about $100 million, through recommendations by the Secretary of Labor. *New York Times,* April 17, 1968. Earlier reviews of Job Corps experience had indicated high costs and low retention rates. See Sar A. Levitan, *The Great Society's Poor Law,* Policy Studies in Employment and Welfare no. 1 (Baltimore: Johns Hopkins Press, 1969), Chapter 13, especially pp. 285–288, 296–298.

11 A later revision reduced this total to 11 million, suggesting the difficulty of estimating numbers of these magnitudes. The "out of the labor force" figure was estimated on the basis of poor persons between the ages of 14 and 64, excluding those still in school, handicapped, or required in the home. For the revised 11-million figure, see *Manpower Report of the President,* January 1969, pp. 141–142.

"hard-core" unemployed in the fifty cities where the National Alliance of Businessmen's JOBS program is concentrated. While this subgroup is important, there is growing recognition of the fact that many "disadvantaged" are working hard in low-paid and often dead-end jobs—nearly 6 million. The opportunity to get training that would prepare them for better jobs, with subsidies to offset the loss of income during training, should be offered to this larger group through MDTA institutional training, adult vocational education, possibly subsidized on-the-job training, and public service employment. While the percentage of nonwhites among the working poor is higher than for whites, the *absolute* number of whites in this group (over 11 million) is much larger than nonwhites (less than 2 million)—a fact often forgotten in the concern with providing training and employment opportunities for nonwhites.

Lack of Effective Coordination at the Federal Level

Various manpower programs administered by the Department of Labor were in separate bureaus before the Manpower Administartion was given greater responsibility in 1967. But a number of manpower programs are outside the jurisdiction of the department. It was noted at the outset of the preceding section that some manpower-type programs are in the Department of Health, Education, and Welfare. For example, vocational education programs for out-of-school adults, vocational rehabilitation of physically handicapped (and now others), and adult basic education (to remedy prior deficiencies) are funded and administered by HEW. The vocational rehabilitation program in particular has many of the components of an adequate manpower program: guidance, training, medical care, counseling, and follow-up, which are often lacking in other programs.[12] The Community Action Programs (CAPS) of the Office of Economic Opportunity, the Job Corps, and VISTA (domestic service corps) also have manpower components, yet there was separate OEO administration until the transfer of the Job Corps to the Department of Labor early in 1969. The Department of Commerce administers the Economic Development Administration, successor to the Area Redevelopment Administration, which has manpower implications, as does the new Model Cities Program of the Department of Housing and Urban Development.

In addition to major programs in separate Federal departments, there are the military training programs of the Department of Defense, the efforts to train men being demobilized,[13] and the manpower implications of draft policy

12 See Garth L. Magnum and Lowell M. Glenn, *Vocational Rehabilitation and Federal Manpower Policy,* Policy Papers in Human Resources and Industrial Relations no. 6 (Ann Arbor, 1968; published jointly with the National Manpower Policy Task Force). The lack of coordination between vocational education programs and information on the labor market available through the U.S. Employment Service and local offices is pointed out by Gerald G. Somers, "The Response of Vocational Education to Labor Market Changes," *Journal of Human Resources* 3, Supplement (1968): 32–58.

13 Some have presumably acquired skills useful in civilian work, but others have not. See "Jobs for Ex-GI's: Companies Cooperate with Services to Train Men Nearing Discharge," *Wall Street Journal,* May 14, 1968. This manpower retraining problem will grow as the Vietnam commitment tapers off and more servicemen seek civilian employment. For a discussion of experience and possibilities for further programs, see Robert B. Richardson, *Transferring Military Experience to Civilian Jobs,* U.S. Department of Labor, Manpower Administration, 1969.

for the supply of scarce skills. The federal government itself has many training programs, not always well coordinated, and its demand for high-talent people is growing.

Finally, if "education" contributes to the development of manpower, as it unquestionably does, then it is clear that educational policies do not mesh well with manpower policies. Young people are educated, but not always for the world of work. The transition from school to work is faulty because less attention is often given noncollege youth; vocational education in the past has generally not been related to expanding occupations; and guidance counseling has been inadequate.[14] The failure of the school system in these respects has made remedial manpower training programs necessary, but there is practically no coordination between the two.

Can all of these separate programs be coordinated at the federal level? The President's Committee on Manpower, with representatives from each of the relevant departments, made an attempt in 1966 and 1967. It had an energetic executive director, a limited staff, and accomplished something. It initiated the concept of a Concentrated Employment Program (CEP) in a number of large cities, but the "delivery system" was weak in many.[15] The Cabinet Committee is now dead.

14 See Rupert N. Evans, Garth L. Magnum, and Otto Pragan, *Education for Employment,* Policy Papers in Human Resources and Industrial Relations no. 14 (Ann Arbor, 1969), especially pp. 44–60.

15 For a candid review of this experience, see R. Thayne Robson, "Administering Federal Manpower Programs," *Proceedings of the Twentieth Annual Meeting,* Industrial Relations Research Association, December 1967, pp. 182–189. On the same point, see also Garth L. Magnum, "Evaluating Federal Manpower Programs," ibid., pp. 161–171.

Meanwhile, in the last 1968 session of Congress the Republicans introduced a bill providing for a new cabinet-level Department of Education and Manpower. It was not considered then, but it has the support of the Advisory Commission on Vocational Education, which made its report before passage of the Vocational Education Act of 1968, as well as of influential Congressmen and professional educators.

There may be something to be said for this proposal, but opponents are concerned that the educational establishment (now in HEW) would dominate manpower programs. An alternative and better proposal is for a comprehensive manpower act, which would authorize manpower services "structured along functional rather than program lines so as to lend themselves to tailoring according to community and individual need." There would be overall funding, but the amount of money allocated to each service or function would not be fixed. Better coordination would be achieved if federal funds were appropriated to one agency, possibly an expanded Manpower Administration.[16] If that is not possible, funds for use by the manpower agency should be earmarked in appropriations for education, health, military demobilization, and other manpower-related programs that are included in the budgets of other government depart-

[16] These suggestions have been developed by Garth L. Magnum in his study of federal manpower programs. Magnum has called it to my attention that Congress moved in this direction in December 1967 when it amended Title I-B of the Economic Opportunity Act to allow comingling of the Neighborhood Youth Corps, Mainstream, and New Careers under a local prime sponsor, although guidelines were not issued at that time.

ments or agencies. The manpower agency could then apply for funds from these agencies for specific manpower training and supporting activities.

The reorganization of the Manpower Administration announced by President Nixon in March 1969, following recommendations by Secretary of Labor George P. Shultz, is based on the assumption that federal funding by categories will be supplanted (if Congress approves) by block grants or overall funding in response to coordinated manpower programs proposed by states and cities through the new regional manpower administrations.[17] If so, the point discussed in the next section may indicate the way toward a solution.

Weaknesses in the Delivery System at the State and Local Levels

Many states have apparently not been able to plan and deliver manpower programs on a statewide basis. The lack of acceptable state agencies[18] and the seriousness of man-

17 Subsequently, President Nixon sent a message on manpower training to the Congress on August 12, 1969. At the same time, the administration bill, known as the Manpower Training Act of 1969, was introduced with a letter from Secretary of Labor Shultz to the Congress stating that "the proposal will establish a comprehensive manpower development program to assist persons in overcoming obstacles to suitable employment." A detailed review of the bill is beyond the scope of this paper. Two other bills, one by Congressman Steiger (R) of Wisconsin and Congressman O'Hara (D) of Michigan, have also been introduced. Despite the hope that some comprehensive new manpower legislation would be passed in 1970, the Conference Committee bill emerging from the Congress was vetoed by the President, for a number of specific reasons.

18 Apparently the State Employment Service agencies, as part of the USES, were not considered adequate to handle programs for the disad-

power problems in the large cities led both the Office of Economic Opportunity and the Manpower Administration to bypass states and make grants directly to city groups. This was particularly true for the community action agencies funded by OEO. But these local agencies also depended on other sources of federal funding, sometimes from the Department of Labor and sometimes from Health, Education, and Welfare. And they could not always deal with the government just at the departmental level; there were separate but related programs, funded individually and with their own applications and standards, administered separately by a staff in Washington.

It was no wonder, then, that frustration and confusion developed at the local level. Few cities had developed a Human Resources Administration as New York City did in 1966, and even here complaints about the problems created by multiple sources of federal funding were loud and forceful. In other cities, it was not uncommon to hear about federally funded programs being carried out in ignorance of other similar or related programs.

An effort to get better coordination at the local level was made under the Cooperative Area Manpower Planning System (CAMPS) developed within the past two years, but it is too early to determine its effectiveness. In the meantime, the administration bill, the Manpower Training Act

---

vantaged. However, they have been moving in the direction of providing more services and presumably will be asked to do even more under the new Manpower Administration reorganization and under proposed legislation. The question of which agency will be the prime sponsor for state and local manpower programs under new legislation is likely to be a controversial one.

of 1969, includes the provision that each state and each large metropolitan area (SMSA—which sometimes crosses state lines) be required to prepare an annual multiyear plan for use of federal funds. The planning organization might be an incorporated CAMPS group. But planning and operating functions should be separate and should relate manpower programs to those in education, regional development, housing, and transportation.

Should there be a *single* local operating agency receiving and spending funds for manpower services to the individual? A strong case can be made for such an agency, with many branches throughout a large metropolitan area. An earlier proposal was to make the Employment Service the "one-stop manpower services" agency.[19] Here an individual seeking work could be interviewed and counseled, given assistance if health services were required, given training, referred to jobs, and followed up on the job. Some of these services could be provided by the Employment Service directly; others could be contracted for with other agencies, as in health services and training. While the Employment Service has been expanding its services and the concept of its mission, it still does not appear to have the full confidence of employers or of job applicants, particularly in the black community.[20] Perhaps it can change further under

19 This was the phrase used in the report of the Employment Service Task Force, published in the *Employment Service Review* (U.S. Department of Labor), February 1966, pp. 1–37. The chairman of the Task Force was George P. Shultz, former Secretary of Labor and now Director, Office of Management and Budget.

20 For examples of this distrust and reports of some Employment Service success in overcoming it, see Michael E. Carbine, "Communi-

the pressure of funds granted for specific functions. But it is probable that other community agencies will be developed for professional delivery of manpower services, as Community Action programs have been developed with the help of the Employment Service in a number of cities.[21] It is to be hoped that the reorganization of the Manpower Administration, mentioned earlier, will push more responsibility onto the regional and local manpower agencies. But it will still require more *local* effort at coordination of many separate groups and agencies, and this has not yet occurred in many areas.

The Problem of Community Control of Manpower Programs

Community action agencies under past OEO programs have had the authority to hire nonprofessionals from disadvantaged groups, often those previously without work, to help in outreach programs, initial interviewing and screening, and some counseling. They have also sought to involve

---

cating with the Disadvantaged," *Manpower* (U.S. Department of Labor, Manpower Administration), 1 (October 1969): 3–6.

21 Experience with these CAP agencies varies. One study of the Boston agency known as ABCD raised the question of whether it should try to find jobs that the disadvantaged could not find on their own and pointed to its limited success in finding better-paying jobs. See Peter B. Doeringer et al., "Low-Income Labor Markets and Urban Manpower Programs: A Critical Assessment," a report submitted to the U.S. Department of Labor, Office of Manpower Research, by Harvard University, Cambridge, Massachusetts, January 1969. On the other hand, it is my impression that the Boston program is one of the better ones. The conclusion that the agency failed to find good-paying jobs for more than one-third of the placements is hardly a major criticism of the agency; it reflects labor-market conditions.

community representatives in planning and approving programs. In some cities, formal and informal community groups have sought to control the allocation of funds for manpower and related services, and in at least one instance these groups have been able to mobilize political pressures to secure greater allocations of funds from the federal manpower programs.

This issue is not unrelated to the efforts of community groups in large cities to exercise more control over the schools in their areas. If programs are designed to help the "disadvantaged in the central cities," they may be expected to want some voice in the development and administration of local programs. But racial conflict and confusion result when there are no clear-cut guidelines on the responsibilities of the professional citywide delivery agency vis-à-vis groups seeking to represent the recipients of manpower services. Federal funds cannot be turned over without restrictions or limits to be administered and spent by representatives of community members receiving services.

These services must be organized and provided by professionally trained, qualified people, augmented by new recruits who receive appropriate training. Parenthetically, the shortage of competent and sensitive manpower specialists has probably exacerbated the demand for community control. Community representation through the hiring and training of subprofessional and nonprofessional administrative staffs is appropriate; community *control* of funds is not. Community advisory boards can provide a necessary channel to and from the agency and the community.[22] Profes-

22 For an analysis of this experience, see Levitan, *The Great Society's Poor Law,* Chapter 3.

sional administrators ignore this channel at their peril, but they must also resist movements to take over decision making under federal funding.

Federal Financing of Private Training and Job-Development Efforts

The Manpower Administration's MA-4 and MA-5 programs provide subsidies in the form of contracts to firms that agreed under the National Alliance of Businessmen's JOBS program to hire specific numbers of "hard core unemployed."[23] The NAB drive, spearheaded by state and city committees under the leadership of Henry Ford II, aimed for commitments to hire 100,000 by July 1, 1969, and a total of 500,000 by July 1, 1971, in the 50 largest cities.[24] Many firms have made the commitment without asking for a federal subsidy; some have contracts providing subsidies for training periods of 12 to 52 weeks, which averaged between $2500 and $5000 per trainee in one large city.

The anticipated average training subsidy in the planning stages nationally was around $3500. This included not only actual on-the-job training costs, but preemployment remedial education, preemployment training, sensitivity train-

[23] The Manpower Administration of the Department of Labor has defined this group to include "poor persons who do not have suitable employment and who are either (1) school dropouts; (2) under 22 years of age; (3) 45 years of age or over; (4) handicapped; or (5) subject to special obstacles to employment." "Request for Proposal," MA-3, 1968. By September 1969 some 990 contracts had been signed.
[24] The Nixon administration proposes to expand the 50-city program to 125 cities under the new NAB chairman, Donald M. Kendall. *Manpower* 1 (April 1969). See also "Nixon Urges Rise in Aid to Jobless," *New York Times,* March 16, 1969. The July 1971 target was subsequently raised to 600,000 jobs.

ing for supervisors, and the like. Some of this is contracted out to the private consulting firms that have sprung up to provide services to participating firms, for a fee that becomes part of the firm's subsidy. While these costs may seem high, there is at least the possibility that in some cases they are not high enough, considering the special problems of bringing the really disadvantaged to acceptable standards of productive performance, including observance of plant rules and discipline. Supervisors, union representatives, and even fellow employees have to adjust to new problems and also require some training. Furthermore, promotional opportunities must be taken into account, as they have in some cases with union participation and pressure.

It may still be too early to evaluate the effectiveness of partnership between the federal government and private industry as an approach to this problem, but there is no doubt that the private commitment to solving it is now substantial.[25] If the Nixon administration should later take

25 For a detailed account of one company's involvement and learning experience, see the summary of a speech by Virgil E. Boyd, president of the Chrysler Corporation, *New York Times,* June 11, 1968. A comprehensive account of business efforts is reported in "Dealing the Negro In," *Business Week,* May 4, 1968, pp. 64–84 (a *Business Week* "Special Report"). A more recent review of the NAB program is found in Joseph A. Loftus, "Business and Government Move to Expand Job Training Plan," *New York Times,* February 3, 1969, and an extensive analysis is found in Sar A. Levitan, Garth L. Mangum, and Robert Taggart III, *Economic Opportunity in the Ghetto: The Partnership of Government and Business,* Policy Studies in Employment and Welfare no. 3 (Baltimore: Johns Hopkins Press, 1969; published jointly with the National Manpower Policy Task Force), especially Chapter 2, "Policy Studies in Employment and Welfare." For a study of pre-MA-3 on-the-job training programs, see Chapter 3 of the present work.

a different approach, through tax incentives (credits) rather than contractual subsidies, new questions will arise. Who will determine when a tax credit will be given for a training program and how much? A flat percentage, such as the one used to encourage capital investment, will run the risk of rewarding a firm for doing training that it is already doing. And the cost in terms of lost tax revenues would be greater than the subsidy cost, unless it is proposed that there be no federal standards or personnel to monitor the extent to which taxpayers are getting their money's worth.[26] Tax matters, furthermore, are administered by the Internal Revenue Service, which is not equipped to evaluate job training programs or their success in retaining and promoting new employees.

An alternative to financial inducements to private employers to hire the disadvantaged is to provide similar inducements to locate new plants in the core cities. This has been done with two firms in the Roxbury area of Boston, one in Minneapolis, and one in Rochester, New York.[27] These "experiments" are too new for evaluation, but they do not offer the prospect of large-scale employment. The issue of community control will come up here also; management of the new firms cannot be of the "plantation type."[28] As in less-developed countries, the challenge is to provide

[26] For a perceptive comparison of subsidies versus tax credits in manpower programs, see Lester C. Thurow, "Tax Credits for Training the Disadvantaged," multilith, a report prepared for the Urban Coalition and the Brookings Institution (Washington, D.C., 1969).

[27] For a review of several cases, see Levitan, Mangum, and Taggart, *Economic Opportunity in the Ghetto,* Chapter 3.

[28] " 'Plantationship' Seen in Job Aid: Negro Businessman Asks for Slum 'Partnership,' " *New York Times,* April 7, 1968.

training and advancement opportunities to the local people, including eventual management of these enterprises.

Guaranteed Employment versus Guaranteed Income

Proposals for a guaranteed income for poor people, in the form of a negative income tax to replace present welfare payments and provide a minimum family income, have had strong support from the academic community. At least one "experiment" has been mounted with federal support in New Jersey to determine how such incomes are spent and their effect on the incentive to work or to prepare for employment.

For present welfare recipients who cannot work because they are infirm, aged, have small children at home, or for other reasons, the concept of a guaranteed income as an alternative to welfare payments has much to commend it. But for those who are in the poverty group because they are unemployed, intermittently employed, or have low-paying jobs, employment rather than guaranteed income is better and has wider public support. The report of the so-called tripartite Automation Commission in 1966 included a recommendation for "government as an employer of last resort."[29] Public service employment was proposed in 1968 in two bills introduced by Senator Clark of Pennsylvania and Congressman O'Hara of Michigan. While these were not passed, Congress did amend the Social Security Act in 1967 to require that federally supported relief recipients

[29] *Technology and the American Economy,* Report of the National Commission on Technology, Automation, and Economic Progress, Washington, D.C., February 1966.

(unless specifically excused) would be trained for jobs or provided public sector employment in a new Work Incentive program (WIN) to be administered by the Department of Labor.[30]

What kinds of public sector jobs would be useful, especially for those who cannot make it in private employment? Under the New Careers Program, some thousands of indigenous poor people have been hired as nonprofessionals or aides in teaching, day-care centers, health and welfare centers, and other neighborhood services in the Community Action programs administered by OEO. So far, the New Careers program has not been as successful as proponents had predicted.

Similar public service jobs have been suggested in other fields, such as police, public construction, sanitation, and the like, but these are likely to run into the opposition of professionals, civil service personnel, or skilled workers who fear job dilution or competition. Despite these difficulties, there are probably 1.5 million people who could be usefully employed in the public sector if financing were available.[31]

[30] One report claimed that this program had "moved 50,000 welfare recipients into jobs or training programs in the 6 months ending June 6, 1969." *Manpower* 1 (August 1969): 9.

[31] Garth L. Mangum, "Practical Consequences of Guaranteeing Employment," paper prepared for the U.S. Chamber of Commerce (Washington, D.C., 1968). The same point has been made more strongly by Harold L. Sheppard in a staff paper for the W. E. Upjohn Institute for Employment Research, "The Nature of the Job Problem and the Role of New Public Service Employment" (Kalamazoo, Mich., 1969), especially pp. 22–25. Sheppard estimates that nearly half of unfilled needs could be met by nonprofessional applicants.

The WPA experience in the 1930s was not all useless "make-work," as it is so often pictured. Highways and roads were improved, bridges built, sidewalks and curbs laid, public buildings constructed, and parks and playgrounds developed, along with many other civil improvements that we now enjoy. These did cost federal tax money but gave millions at least temporary employment. Similar construction today requires local property-tax money and is done through private contractors or city or town departments. There are other necessary jobs in state and local governments which might be filled by federally financed job-creation programs, possibly through subsidies to employing units, as in the private sector NAB-JOBS program. So the "net cost" of public employment through federal funding is always likely to be lower than the amount of the appropriation. And if nonprofit employment were also subsidized, as in hospitals, for example, lower relative costs to patients would offset part of the employment subsidy. The Clark and O'Hara bills (mentioned earlier) proposed $10.3 billion over four years and $4 billion for one year, respectively. High as these are, they are less than the costs of the proposed negative income tax, which range from $5 to $10 billion annually, and in some proposals even more.[32]

There is, however, one major problem in much public service employment. The management skills necessary to employ the disadvantaged are not found as much in government agencies as in private industry. Unless acceptable standards of performance are demanded, the productivity

[32] See George H. Hildebrand, "Second Thoughts on the Negative Income Tax," *Industrial Relations* 6 (February 1967): 138–154.

level of public service employment is likely to be much less than in the private sector. There is the further difficulty that public service jobs may be "dead-end," rather than entry jobs on a promotion ladder. In short, while public service employment has much to commend it over a guaranteed income plan alone, it is not an easily developed alternative to manpower training and services that prepare people for competitive employment in the private and nonprofit sectors. Public agencies that operate under civil service recruitment and advancement procedures pose a further obstacle unless entry requirements are made more flexible. Despite these problems, however, the possibility of expanding public service employment as an alternative to guaranteed incomes deserves more attention than it has received recently.

Interrelationships of Manpower and Other Urban Programs

The relationship between manpower programs and improving the ghetto schools has already been suggested. Deficiencies in Southern schools, both urban and rural, as well as in many ghetto schools have required the kinds of remedial education and basic training that federal manpower programs have provided. Clearly, state and federal financing of improvements in education in these areas will be required, simply because the cities and towns lack the financial ability and often the commitment to make real improvements. Despite some questions as to its efficacy, a Head Start Program for preschool children makes sense as a part of improved education.

But this is only one subsystem of a larger system needed to deal effectively with the urban crisis. Improvement in health and medical care in the central cities is essential, as the manpower programs for the disadvantaged have discovered. Medical and physical disabilities (including cases of drug addiction) have handicapped the placement of some of the disadvantaged no less than they have those with physical handicaps due to industrial or nonindustrial accidents. The latter have been the special beneficiaries of a generous federal-state vocational rehabilitation program.

Slum housing and the inability of many to find low-cost housing in the industrial suburbs surrounding central cities have also militated against job placement and the likelihood that those who are placed will become responsible and committed employees. If residents of the ghettos find jobs in the suburbs, they still have the problem of transportation. Few have their own automobiles, and most are dependent on public transportation. One example is Watts, whose residents must travel by several bus routes for as much as three hours a day to and from employment elsewhere in the Los Angeles area. In Boston the public transportation authority started in June 1968 an "Employment Express" bus route (now discontinued) from the primarily black Roxbury area to the plants along the Route 128 semicircle in the Boston suburbs.[33] Partly because of manpower pro-

33 Initial reports claimed that between 150 and 200 people secured jobs along Route 128 as a result of the express bus. *Boston Herald Traveler*, June 6, 1968, and *Business Week*, August 24, 1968, p. 86. Unpublished data available on a weekly basis through the MBTA showed that the number of riders had been dropping, but the reasons were not given. A subsequent analysis concluded that about 122 persons found jobs be-

grams, improvements in public transportation from central to satellite cities is clearly needed.

Some of the problems of the central cities have been the result of migration from the rural areas and small towns of the South. As improvements such as more favorable welfare payments are made in the central cities, the inducement to migration may be expected to increase. It may seem that a simple answer would be to provide employment opportunities where the disadvantaged still live—in the rural South and possibly in Puerto Rico. But we know that migration cannot be prevented within the political limits of the United States, and a combination of economic and political factors may account for the forced migration of blacks from the Deep South.[34] So while better regional development may stem migration somewhat, it is not the only part of the system that needs attention, for the rising population in the central cities is now owing more to increases in births than to in-migration.[35]

In summary, this section has indicated the system interrela-

---

cause of this program, and 92 were still working. "Many persons who initially used the bus service subsequently bought cars or joined car pools. Some also found it difficult to meet varying shift schedules or work overtime because of fixed bus schedules, and in some cases the $2.20 starting wage was not enough better than central city jobs to compensate for the cost and time of the round-trip bus." Carol S. Greenwald and Richard Syron, "Increasing Job Opportunities in Boston's Urban Core," *New England Economic Review* (Federal Reserve Bank of Boston), January–February 1969, pp. 30–40.

[34] See Michael J. Piore, "Negro Workers in the Mississippi Delta: Problems of Displacement and Adjustment," *Proceedings of the Twentieth Annual Winter Meeting,* Industrial Relations Research Association, December 1967, pp. 366–374.

[35] Killingsworth, *Jobs and Income for Negroes,* pp. 47–48.

tionships between manpower programs, education, housing, transportation, investment in ghetto businesses, and rural development. Manpower and related programs have already been fragmented among several federal departments, and the other programs are often either the responsibility of different agencies or the concern of none. Possibly the Model Cities program in the Department of Housing and Urban Development is intended to deal with these related problems under a single program, although subsequent developments have made it seem doubtful. The Nixon administration faces either a continuation or a revitalization of this effort, unless the decision is made to emasculate it.

Conclusions

The major conclusions and final observations in this brief review of a complex and changing field may be summarized as follows:[36]

1. Our present federally financed manpower programs are not equal to the need, even though their expansion in recent years has been rapid and the present administration has promised to devote more resources to such programs. Reasonably full employment is essential if training efforts are to succeed, and the current, understandable preoccupation with reducing inflationary pressures must tread a fine line between this objective and the risk of accentuating the problems of training and employing the disadvantaged in our society.

[36] While I should not wish to commit him to the above conclusions, I note that some of these points were made by former Secretary of Labor George P. Shultz in a paper for this volume, drawn from a talk he gave before becoming Secretary, "Issues for Manpower's Action Programs."

2. Past programs have been plagued by lack of coordination at the federal level. Reorganization of the manpower programs in the Department of Labor has tried to deal with these problems internally, and the last reorganization is a step in the right direction. But the problems of interdepartmental coordination, with which the President's Cabinet Committee on Manpower (now expired) sought to deal, are likely to remain. It is to be hoped that the administration's concern for effective coordination and efficient administration will make some progress here. The proposed Manpower Training Act of 1969 includes some provisions for coordination between labor and HEW.

3. In the past, well-intentioned federal programs have foundered at the state and local levels through an inadequate delivery system. Implementation at the local level was sometimes faulty, and recently it has on occasion been characterized by loose fiscal administration. The March 1969 reorganization of the Manpower Administration is intended to strengthen the delivery system to the states and cities, but it is too soon to say whether it will succeed. Much depends on how well they respond, and how effectively the Secretary of Labor moves to correct inadequate proposals and programs.

4. Community control of manpower programs raises some serious questions about the power local groups seek over the expenditure of federal funds. There is an important difference between local groups proposing and advising on a comprehensive local manpower program adapted to local needs and their occasional demands for unrestricted use of funds made available from Washington. Professional supervision

and control of manpower programs at the local level is no less essential than it is at the federal level, but it must be responsive to community objectives. Often the problem is: Who speaks for the community?

5. Federal financing of the National Alliance of Businessmen's JOBS program is one of the more promising recent programs. It is built on the realization that most training takes place on the job rather than off the job and that if top management is committed to hiring the disadvantaged, others in the management group will pitch in rather than drag their feet. The commitment seems to be serious in an increasing number of firms, although it is somewhat disturbing that probably more firms have "signed the pledge" than have signed MA contracts. So it is difficult to determine just how many truly disadvantaged have been hired in this program, as opposed to the practice by those whose pledges cannot be evaluated of "creaming" the better-qualified. Whether promotional opportunities are really being made available for the future is still undetermined, although it is clear that the program has led to a reevaluation of personnel policies and supervisory training programs in a number of firms.

6. Present interest in guaranteed income programs, whether of the negative income tax or family allowances variety, neglects the widespread public concern for improving employment opportunities for those who can work. Public service employment opportunities need to be expanded for those who cannot find jobs in the private sector. Federally subsidized programs in the public sector similar to the NAB-JOBS program is one possibility; application to non-

profit institutions such as hospitals is another. Direct public service employment similar to the old WPA has attractions, since it would conserve local tax money if properly administered. But one drawback is that the management skills necessary for such administration are not widely available or easily developed in many public agencies at all levels of government.

7. Finally, the interrelationship of manpower programs and other federal efforts to deal with the urban crisis deserve emphasis. Manpower programs are only part of a "total system" and taken alone may accentuate some of the problems of the cities. Policy makers are confronted with the consequences of piecemeal efforts, and they need to develop a policy based on an analysis of where federal action is likely to have the greatest positive impact. Despite some allegations to the contrary, however, it is hard to accept any conclusion that puts manpower problems low on the priority list.

2

Issues for Manpower's Action Programs

George P. Shultz

The surge of prosperity in the decade of the sixties brought into sharp focus the difficulty of dealing with problems of black unemployment and underemployment, particularly for teenagers and young adults. Strong efforts to work at the problem have led to greater understanding and have enlarged the pool of ideas on which action programs may draw. But if something has been learned, that something also reveals the complexity of the problem and how much about it is still unknown. This article explores a few issues and ideas that, I hope, will have practical significance.

Principles for Action Programs

The principles I shall suggest are, in one sense, simply personal assertions. At the same time I believe the experience of the recent past offers some evidence in their favor.

1. Income should, if possible, come through jobs. It is essential that people work at something, contribute something of value to society, and be paid for it. I would ask, then, whether a particular program is job-oriented, as distinct from income-oriented, even when the income is provided through what may be a drastic alteration of the welfare system.

Editor's Note: This essay was adapted from Mr. Shultz's talk to the Conference on Race and Unemployment held at the University of Chicago in 1968. Thus it does not reflect his experience as Secretary of Labor or as Director of the Office of Management and Budget. In particular, it does not reflect the recent proposals to decategorize manpower programs, share federal revenues with the states, and reorganize the domestic side of the federal government.

2. The centers of implementation should be reasonably small in size. Large networks of large centers mean bureaucracy. I do not think of that term as one of abuse, but with a large administering group the creativity necessary for success in this area is too often stifled. The exciting programs, the ones that have demonstrated progress, have been relatively small. If they are individually too small to cope with this large problem, we can consider programs that generate many small centers in which many small groups can use their own energy and initiative.

3. Private groups, both profit and nonprofit, should be drawn heavily into the action, as they increasingly are—at last. Government must be strongly involved, too, but governmental programs should seriously attend to patterns of collaboration among various groups. The comparative advantage of one group or another must be studied in order to discern which kinds of collaboration will pay off in terms of solutions.

4. We should be realistic about the brass-tacks aspects of every proposal. The bloom is off the rose of many "bold, imaginative programs" because they were started without a clear conception of the potential problems involved in making them work and without a plan for dealing with these problems. People have come down to earth, and a very good thing, for the difficulties of implementation are many, and only with realism can one hope to carry one's organization through them.

5. The question must be asked of every program: Is it sharply focused on the problem group? I am distressed at the broad range of governmental and private programs in

which people have gradually slipped away from the main objective. This is very easy to do, and it is simple enough to understand how and why it happens, since it is really only a matter of following the path of least resistance. For that reason, every program should include some mechanism to assure as far as possible that appropriated money, effort, and other resources are and will stay directed at the people about whom we are most worried.

6. There should be a flavor of experimentation and variety in action programs. This is particularly important in the long run, but it has application in the short run as well. While there may be no big new programs or major appropriations in the current fiscal year, we shall see much effort expended as a result of the thrust of current programs. Diversity among programs will be valuable, because while we may make strong assertions in favor of this or that program, we do not really know how any program will work. There is much to be learned, and there should be means developed for judging what has worked and what has failed. It is important also to stick with programs, to allow them to come to fruition. One of our problems in manpower work has been that something is started, it goes for a while, it suffers reverses, appropriations are cut, then suddenly it is out of business and another one has been started. Time is needed to allow for a true test of effectiveness.

Programs and Issues for the Private Sector

The great variety of action programs, existing or proposed, for alleviating unemployment problems can be classed roughly in these categories: (1) government manpower programs, including suggestions about their organization and measures to enlist the private sector in educational and employment processes; (2) developments in the field of formal education; (3) programs concerned with discrimination; (4) programs concerned with the ghetto itself, including ways to make it possible for people to leave the ghetto if they wish.

There has been a marked acceleration in the development of programs that would involve the private sector in an attack on unemployment. This promising development implies government stimulus to business performance. But while enlistment of the private sector may be fruitful, it also raises many issues of its own. Because of the importance of the potential contributions of the private sector and the difficulties that action programs may encounter in this sphere, the following remarks concentrate on four issues of central concern to the private effort.

Issues of the Workplace

With programs involving the private sector in mind, I see as the first set of issues those of the workplace. We have hardly given this side of the problem the careful thought that it deserves. Remember, we are talking about the idle, unemployed teenager—difficult to handle—and proposing to bring *him into* shops, unions, and offices throughout the country.

What about discipline? The person we are talking about is likely to be more tardy, more absent, more prone to conflict, and in general more difficult to bring to a productive level of work. What should be done if someone is repeatedly late? Absent? Difficult? Unproductive? If treatment of everyone is evenhanded, our new employee will not last long. The problem will hardly be solved; it will hardly have been met. On the other hand, to ignore obvious and repeated violations of rules means the likelihood of deterioration in standards throughout the workplace.

Obviously, this is an issue on which union and company must talk very carefully before instituting a program. It is not only, or even especially, the president of the United Auto Workers and the president of the Ford Motor Company who should be involved; plant managers and local presidents, stewards and foremen must discuss the problems and plan to meet them, including in their plans measures to gain the acceptance of rank-and-file workers.

There is much to be said for a consortium of firms working on the problem along these lines. Under such a consortium, an employee could be released from one firm but not from the system of firms; he may be given a new start at another firm. The experience might constitute a kind of education, especially if it is thought through and organized in a way that makes it possible to maintain reasonable standards of performance in each shop.

Another issue of the workplace concerns the probationary period. The median probationary period in most international union contracts is about thirty days. During the first thirty days, an employer can fire without reference to normal disciplinary procedures; after thirty days the employee is protected as a full-fledged worker. The rules are devised for the ordinary person entering the stream of employment. When the category of the person entering changes, should the probationary period be changed for everyone, if for anyone?

Nothing is more sacrosanct than seniority. Yet many people just entering a particular work situation under some special programs could have been there five years earlier, had they had the chance. Should they begin at the bottom of the ladder? When it comes to layoffs, will they be among the first to go, or will some special provisions insulate them from the normal rules of the game? There will be questions about whatever is done, and no questions stir matters up as much as those involving seniority.

These and many other issues must be faced in the workplace. They cannot be ignored, for to do so will doom any program to failure before it even starts.

Issues of Comparative Advantage

Consider such functions as outreach, literacy training, acculturation to the discipline of work, skill training, placement, and guidance. Against these functions consider the agencies that might undertake them: private employers, publicly and privately supported nonprofit groups, unions, schools, various levels and agencies of government.

The questions of comparative advantage involve the determination of who can best do what kind of function. Employers are not very effective at things like outreach. Government is not very effective either. The best job seems likely to be done by the nonprofit, indigenous groups in the neighborhoods who are part and parcel of the situation. They are able to reach out, find the people, and perform the first steps of getting an individual started at work. For many aspects of work training itself, private employers seem best equipped, but schools and various nonprofit or government groups may do better at some of the other necessary functions. Furthermore, an effective program for an individual will include several of these functions, so that the myriad problems of cooperative and productive relations among the groups involved come quickly to the fore. Again, these are issues to be thought through and worked out with care.

Issues of Financing

A variety of methods for financing has been proposed; the differences among them have clear implications for the way programs would be organized and administered. No matter what method of government finance is adopted, private money will inevitably be involved, at least in terms of the commitment of talented manpower to the administration of programs and of organizational problems associated with their implementation.

The President's Commission on Civil Disorders suggested that employers be given tax credits for employing each person in a designated group, howeved defined. The commission said that this method is supported by employers, who are already accustomed to working through tax incentives, and that it has the advantage of being simple and direct. But standards for qualification and performance would almost inevitably be administered by the Treasury or the Internal Revenue Service, although this is not exactly their area of comparative advantage. In addition, this method has the disadvantage of further eroding the tax base.

A second method involves annual congressional appropriations with funds being made available either directly by government agencies, as in Manpower Development and Training Act activities, or by contracts between government agencies and private employers or nonprofit organizations. In either case, administration at the federal level would presumably be by an agency specializing in the problems of workers who are hard to find and place, but the method of contracting out would, by involving a multiplicity of points of implementation, encourage experiments and adaptation to local conditions. This is the pattern of the National Alliance of Business program, which has met with initial success and wide acceptance at least in the upper echelons of the business community.

There is a third method of financing that seems very attractive to me but that has been little discussed. It accords well with the concept that people should have greater personal control over their own destinies. This method too calls for annual appropriation of necessary funds by the Congress. But buying power, so to speak, would then be given to individuals, though not necessarily in the form of money. A person could receive credits entitling him to a certain amount of training, counseling, and wage subsidy benefits. It would be up to him to exercise these credits to his best advantage, as in the operation of the GI Bill.

This approach makes people nervous, perhaps because planners think they know more about the problem than the person who is unemployed, but such evidence as we have does not bear out this supposition. Certainly there is much to learn about this type of approach. But I think experimentation with it would be most worthwhile, both with respect to the 19-year-old unemployed dropout and with respect to the school system itself. The expectation would be that new or drastically altered institutions of training would emerge, tailored much more to the needs of the disadvantaged. Alternatively, or concurrently, experimental schools might be established in the ghetto, directly addressing themselves to the problems of their people without reference to the rest of the school system.

In school systems such as that of New York City or Chicago, there are systemwide rules governing pay, job selection, seniority, curriculum, and so on. It is extremely difficult in such contexts to concentrate on the special needs of particular groups of students. It might be feasible to have bidding for a cooperative city-neighborhood private school in a city, to be operated by a non-school-system group. The money would be given explicitly for experimentation on problems of education in the ghetto. In any case, the objective would be a method of finance that placed expanded control of implementation in the hands of the people to be helped and that encouraged an educational program keyed to the area involved.

Issues of Control

Finally, there are issues of freedom and control in the operation of any of these programs. It is desirable to encourage variety, scope, and initiative, to promote conditions in which learning about programs may be maximized. At the same time, local groups, especially the private ones, who would be heavily relied upon, are not accustomed to being overseen in detail on this kind of matter. Since the importance of freedom does not exclude the need for some control, some means of determining the nature of the fulfillment of a contract, I think we can expect much conflict on this issue.

I hope it is apparent from this discussion that the quality of public-private relations will be severely tested in the time ahead. Clearly, government cannot do this job alone, nor, despite the current emphasis on privately operated programs, can private industry. Furthermore, at every turn there are opportunities for stress and strain, suspicion and recrimination, and credit or blame in the interaction of public and private groups. If pragmatic adaptation to the need to solve practical problems is the genius of American government and industry, we can hope that these severe tests will be met. One point is increasingly noted and abundantly clear. The disadvantaged are not alone in having much work to do.

3

Federal Training Programs for Dispersed-Employment Occupations*

David P. Taylor
and Michael J. Piore

A considerable portion of occupational training in the United States is on-the-job training sponsored and supervised by the employer.[1] Federal manpower programs have sought to reinforce this practice through subsidies to employers who provide training in their own establishments.[2] Such subsidies, however, may simply absorb training costs that the employer would have undertaken independently. In this event, the federal programs are uneconomic in that they make no net contribution to the pool of trained manpower.[3] The risk of duplication appears to be least in

* The material reported in this paper was collected under a grant from the Office of Manpower Policy, Evaluation, and Research, U.S. Department of Labor, under the authority of Title I of the Manpower Development and Training Act of 1962. The judgments expressed in this document do not necessarily represent the official position or policy of the Department of Labor. The authors wish to express their appreciation to Dudley Post, who provided research assistance for the printing portion of the study, and to their colleagues at M.I.T. for their insights and critical comments.

1 *Formal Occupational Training of Adult Workers,* U.S. Department of Labor, Manpower Administration, Manpower/Automation Research Monograph no. 2 (Washington, D.C., 1964), Table 11, pp. 43–45.

2 For a summary of this evolution, see *Manpower Report of the President* (Washington, D.C.: Government Printing Office, 1969), pp. 89–95.

3 The program may, of course, be justified on other grounds. Federal intervention might, for example, lead to a more equitable allocation of job opportunities or a more equitable distribution of training costs. The former has, in fact, been an explicit goal of recent policy. Were the redistribution of existing costs and opportunities the only goals of federal policy, however, they could probably be attained more efficiently through other measures. And, indeed, one of the chief attractions of federal training programs as a redistributive measure is that with them it appears possible to avoid the social conflicts that other methods en-

occupations with dispersed employment. In the case of such occupations, the typical firm is small, and trained labor may be pirated from other establishments. The possibility that other employers will pirate workers may deter training even in periods of labor shortage. One would expect to find, therefore, under-investment in human capital in such occupations and a high payoff in federal training programs.

The authors examined three federally financed training programs in labor-shortage occupations where employment is dispersed over a large number of establishments, each of which was small in relation to the total market. These programs provided training for tool and die makers, offset printers, and restaurant cooks and chefs, and all were sponsored by multiestablishment organizations: either employer associations (tool and die, cook-chefs) or trade unions (printers). In the course of the study it became apparent that despite dispersion of employment, strong endogenous patterns of manpower training and utilization made it impossible to assume that the training offered by the federal programs was net. In the light of this finding, the authors concluded that the critical issue facing federally financed training programs was the avoidance of redundancy by measures taken in the design and administration of such programs. The first portion of this paper describes and

---

tail: the redistribution can be financed by the added productivity that the beneficiaries acquire through training rather than through a reduction in the income levels of other members of the labor force. This characteristic of redistribution through training, however, will be realized only if its contribution is net.

analyzes the endogenous training patterns in the three occupations; the second portion considers the question of avoiding substitute training.

Endogenous Training Patterns in Dispersed-Employment Occupations

The study revealed two endogenous patterns of training for tool and die makers, offset printers, and cook-chefs: employer-organized training programs and worker-initiated training by job movement. Worker-initiated training by job movement predominates in the case of cook-chefs. Tool and die makers receive some training in this manner, but they may also receive employer-sponsored training. In the printing trades, training is acquired through programs organized by the employers.

Employer-Organized Training The employer-organized training for printers and for tool and die makers did not differ in essentials from training organized by large enterprises with extensive internal labor markets, which have been documented by other studies.[4] The training takes place largely on the job during the production process. Experienced craftsmen or line supervisors serve as instructors communicating the required skills orally and by demonstration to the trainee, who then perfects them through repetition. The learning process often involves promotion through a sequence of jobs which build in-

[4] See, for example, *Work Force Adjustments in Private Industry—Their Implications for Manpower Policy,* Manpower/Automation Research Monograph no. 7 (Washington, D.C., n.d.). This document contains references to other literature on this subject.

creasingly complex and diversified skills. Alternatively, the supervisor may program the learning process by assigning the trainee a series of tasks that develop his skills in a manner analogous to job promotion. Training during the production process is sometimes preceded by what is called vestibule training. The essential difference between this and other on-the-job training is that demonstration and practice occur in a formal setting established specifically for training purposes.

The federally financed manpower programs for printing and tool and die closely followed the standard on-the-job training patterns. The offset printing training was basically a vestibule program. The tool and die program combined an initial ten-week vestibule program with a second phase of training during the production process. In this second phase, the trainee was hired by employers who agreed in advance to make special training efforts, for which they received a small subsidy. The employer efforts were overseen by a trainer-coach under a system similar to that employed in the restaurant program and described in detail later. The tool and die program also provided, during the ten-week vestibule stage, some formal classroom instruction in mathematics, physics, and tool management. Under normal circumstances, tool and die makers acquire their mathematics and physics in trade school or through correspondence courses; only rarely is it offered in employer-sponsored classes.

The endogenous training patterns in printing and tool and die confronted the federal training programs for these occupations with the same dilemma encountered in training programs for concentrated employment. If the programs operate independently of employers, who control the allocation of labor in the industry, they may end by providing training that the worker cannot utilize, but if the programs are too closely integrated with existing systems of training and allocation, they may end by being redundant, in the sense that the employer would otherwise have paid for the training himself.

The offset printing program was caught on the horns of just this dilemma. The federal program was designed to train journeymen letterpress operators for offset work. With one exception, it was conducted independently of employers. Most trainees were recruited directly by the unions, often with the knowledge of their employers, and only 10 of 29 respondents in a survey of three classes in the program were using their training. Of these 10, moreover, 2 had been offset pressmen before entering the course, 2 became vocational high school teachers, and 1 had been able to benefit from his training only after opening his own shop.[5]

The one close employer link was with the company whose facilities were leased for the program and whose supervisors were hired to conduct it. Eight of the employees of this company were among the program trainees, and the company president admitted that in the absence of federal financing it probably would have provided the training on its own.

[5] A major difficulty was that letterpress operators were also in short supply, and employers preferred to train an offset press operator from scratch rather than lose a letterpress operator.

Since a portion of the tool and die industry is characterized by high turnover and worker-controlled labor allocation, its training program managed to avoid the problems created by independence from employers, but at least two of the large companies hiring program participants sent their own employees into the program and appeared to be using it as a substitute for in-house training.[6]

Given the essential similarity between training in these occupations and training in occupations with concentrated employment, such failings are not surprising. The more interesting analytical problem is the existence of the similarity in the first place, which implies that our initial hypothesis that the concentration of employment was the prime determinant of employer sponsorship was naïve. A comparison of the printing industry with the restaurant industry, in which employers did not sponsor training, suggests two additional factors that determine the pattern of training. The most important of them appears to be specialization of equipment.[7] In the printing industry, where employer sponsorship predominated, shop equipment tends to have peculiarities that make efficient operation a relatively specialized skill. As a result, most workers cannot move easily from shop to shop, turnover is low,

[6] Unfortunately, the response to the mail questionnaire for this program was poor, and it was impossible to determine the full extent to which federal financing was substituting for private funds.

[7] This may be understood in terms of the relation between specialization and the specificity of training. Training on specialized equipment tends to be employer-specific, and this, as Gary Becker has pointed out, gives the employer an incentive to sponsor training. Gary S. Becker, *Human Capital* (New York: National Bureau of Economic Research, 1964), pp. 18–29.

and employers can generally expect a return on investment in training.[8] On the other hand, the restaurant industry, where employers typically do not sponsor training, does not have specialized equipment, and almost all kitchens use roughly the same utensils and machinery. Training is therefore general, and the employer attachment of the labor force is low.[9]

The second factor is feasibility of internal promotion. Most printing establishments are large enough to differentiate jobs in a way that enables workers to learn parts of one job while performing another job lower down the line of progression. The typical restaurant is too small to divide its work in this way: there is not enough work at each skill level to keep a man busy full time. The exceptions in printing appear to confirm this hypothesis. Unusually small shops place a higher premium upon trade-school graduation than their larger competitors, apparently because the lower steps in the natural line of progression are lacking. In the restaurant industry, the exceptions are not so easily reconciled with the hypothesis. One restaurant

8 Thus, for example, of the 29 pressmen responding to the surveys, 13 had worked for their present employer since they became journeymen; 18 had spent at least half their journeyman's career with a single employer; all but 9 had spent at least half their journeyman's career with two or less employers. The median number of years as journeymen was 16; the median years with present employer was 9.

9 Among the restaurants visited for the present study there was one exception, discussed later, where workers apparently entered as kitchen helpers and progressed to chefs. While outsiders could be hired into chef positions, most of the top staff had been trained internally. Highly specialized restaurants (for example, Serbian or Philippine), although not among the establishments in the present study, might also constitute exceptions.

in the study relied heavily upon internal training and promotion from within. Its kitchen, while among the largest, was considerably smaller than the kitchens of several hotels that did not rely on internal promotion. It appears, however, that the discrepancy can be attributed to differences in turnover patterns. Hotel turnover is raised by interior working conditions (irregular hours, notoriously intense heat, and production pressures) to levels that prohibit reliance on internal promotion. Conversely, turnover in the restaurant relying on internal promotion was kept down by its reputation as the region's most fashionable eating place.

Because it exhibits both the restaurant and the printing patterns, tool and die seems to offer the most fruitful source of insights into the determinants of training. Interpretation is complicated, however, by the fact that establishments hiring tool and die trainees did not compose a single industry. Nonetheless, three factors appeared to be responsible for employer sponsorship of training among them. All three factors seemed to be related to size (that is, they were exhibited by establishments with 75 or more employees), although arguably this was coincidental. First, the fringe benefits, seniority rights, and security that large units can offer reduce turnover and hence enable the employer to receive returns on the training he provides. Second, although some large establishments employed only a small number of tool and die makers, they had a large number of machinists, which allowed the formation of an internal line of progression into the toolroom. Finally, there was some indication that employer sponsorship of training is encouraged in establishments producing long runs of standard products, since the narrow training imposed on tool and die makers prevents their skills from being readily transferable.

Worker-Programmed Training The second training pattern that characterizes dispersed employment industries is worker-programmed. Although this pattern applies primarily to restaurant cooks, some tool and die makers follow a similar one.

Through frequent job changes, a cook can program his own on-the-job training, remaining in one establishment only so long as he has something to learn there. Sometimes such movement is vertical, involving heavier responsibility, more skill, or better pay and working conditions. But lateral moves are also frequent. These worker-initiated job changes generate the kind of exposure to new tasks and skills provided elsewhere by movement along an internal line of progression or by supervised rotation of work assignments. On-the-job training is supplemented by formal instruction in specialized proprietary schools. The courses in such schools, however, are not standard, and the trainee must piece together his curriculum from different sources. Some of the chefs interviewed for this study attended classes intermittently for ten or fifteen years. Again, the individual seeks out and evaluates for himself formal educational opportunities that in concentrated occupations are frequently provided by the employer and almost always prescreened by management and brought to the worker's attention by his supervisor.

The locus of initiative and responsibility for training may

be viewed as an instance of a more general phenomenon: those who supply labor take on greater responsibility for the organization and deployment of the work force as the size of the enterprise decreases. Thus, for example, trade unions in large, oligopolistic enterprises tend to be passive, content to restrain or compel managerial activity. Their role contrasts sharply with that of unions in dispersed industries like garments or construction, where the union engages in such activities as the management of health and pension funds, the operation of hiring halls, and the provision of consulting services in areas that elsewhere are defended as the prerogatives of management.

Employer sponsorship of training in the garment industry —or in printing and parts of tool and die, for that matter —indicates, however, that dispersion is not the only variable governing the distribution of market functions. The effect of dispersion is nonetheless instructive: it suggests that other institutions responsible for supplying labor may be able to substitute for the worker and take on the task of programming training when employers abrogate this responsibility. A more extensive study—one, for example, that included construction occupations, where the union does take on part of this task—might have destroyed the strict dichotomy that emerges here between worker programming and employer programming.

A worker who programs his own training must be motivated and resourceful. Advancement is not a function of the particular jobs that people hold; the potential chef holds many of the same jobs as the perpetual kitchen helper. But the would-be chef, unlike the kitchen helper, is alert to opportunities to learn, and when the learning potential of his present position has been exhausted, he is prepared to move to another establishment. The supply of trained labor will thus depend heavily upon the number of workers possessing this trait, and workers who lack it will be penalized more heavily in terms of advancement than those in other occupations.

A second contrast between the training of cook-chefs and that of skilled workers in occupations where employment is concentrated is in the distribution of the cost of formal instruction. Would-be cooks must bear the cost of formal instruction directly, while in occupations where the instruction is provided by the employer, the trainee eithers bears no cost or only an indirect cost, in the form of lower earnings than those available to him in alternative employments. This shift in the cost burden probably tends to exclude from cooks' training workers without financial reserves or who are unable to divert income from consumption. The bias against such workers is probably most pronounced in jobs where training is employer-specific, that is, of no value outside the establishment providing it. Because his training is useful only in his current job, the specifically trained worker can obtain only an unskilled job in the open market. To deter turnover, an employer would have to offer such a worker a wage above the unskilled rate, but he could still pay a wage below the worker's marginal product. And the difference between the wage and the marginal product should serve as an incentive for the employer to invest his own resources in the worker's training. When the training is not employer-specific and can be utilized in a variety of competing establishments, it is widely believed that the employer, because he expects competition to drive up the wage of trained employees until all returns on training are absorbed, will shift the cost of training to the worker.[10] The worker must thus forgo current income to gain access to training, and this should act, like tuition charges, as a deterrent.

Direct tuition charges probably create a bias against those without financial resources, however, even in jobs where the cost of training is ultimately shifted to the labor force. This is so for at least two reasons. First, some workers find it feasible to forgo present consumption if income is deducted at its source, but intolerable if the family must forgo spending the income after receiving it. Second, a critical variable in the decision to invest in training is the rate of interest, which determines the cost of financing training through borrowed funds. It also shows the returns on alternative investments. The higher the rate of interest faced by the individual, therefore, the less likely he is to engage in training. Business firms generally have access to funds at interest rates significantly below those available to the labor force. Thus, even if they pass on the cost of training to the worker, their intervention makes the cost of training lower than when it is borne by the workers directly.

To what extent these factors curtail the supply of cook-chefs depends, of course, upon the relative importance of formal instruction in their acquisition of skills. This cannot be gauged with precision. The 1963 Labor Department survey of occupational training found that 13 percent of all cooks

[10] Becker, *Human Capital,* pp. 8–29.

reported formal training among the ways in which they had learned their job, and 5 percent (nearly three-fifths of whom were trained formally in the army) reported formal training to be the most helpful way.[11] These figures are not large; they imply that even where formal instruction is important, it is secondary to on-the-job training. On the other hand, the total includes a large number of short-order cooks and cooks' helpers. The experienced cooks and chefs interviewed indicated that in the course of their careers they had attended a variety of cooking classes. Such classroom work may be critical to advancement toward the higher levels of the profession.

Cooks' training might conceivably differ from employer-sponsored training in a third respect: the nature of the on-the-job training process and the distribution of its costs. Such differences, however, were not apparent. The essential nature of the process remains the same: skills are absorbed during the process of production by the observation and imitation of experienced craftsmen and are perfected by repetition. The costs of such training include any reduction in the productivity of the chef and his assistant (who is the trainee), wasted raw materials, equipment downtime and damage, and substandard output. The costs are, in other words, reflected in the costs of production. They must thus be borne in the first instance by the employer. If the trainee is to bear them, they must be shifted to him.

There is reason to expect a shift to occur. The high turnover among restaurant employees, which is critical to the training process, also makes it unlikely that the employer

11 *Formal Occupational Training of Adult Workers.*

can capture the increment to productivity that results from training. Thus this increment cannot serve to remunerate the employer for the costs incurred during the training period, and he would be unlikely to tolerate them unless the workers who impose them accept wages below the market level. In addition, not all chefs are equally good instructors. Under some men, a good deal of training occurs, while others provide very little. Clearly, for those wishing to progress in the industry, positions under the former are preferred, and competition for them should force trainees' wages below the market rate.

Such wage differentials should serve the additional purpose of driving nonlearners, who cannot anticipate higher future earnings as a return on current wage sacrifices, from good training positions. This is important because those working in subordinate kitchen positions cover a wide range and include many with no permanent attachment to the restaurant industry and no interest in learning the chef's trade. The preemption by such people of training positions carries an opportunity cost, so that in this case wage differentials perform a social function. It should be noted that this function bears no relation to the costs that training imposes upon the employer. The argument implies that it would be desirable to have good training positions pay below market rates even if training were costless, and there is in fact no reason to expect wage differentials produced by the competition for positions under teaching chefs to correspond to those necessary to compensate the employer for training costs. A wage differential at least sufficient to cover training costs should result from the employer's reluctance to tolerate the training in any other circumstances. But the differential might exceed this lower limit. The cost savings would then presumably be appropriated by the teaching chef.

Several chefs trained abroad spoke of the European market as if it operated (or at least had operated) more or less in this way.[12] Certain restaurants were known throughout the Continent for their great chefs; cooks trained there commanded premium pay, and ambitious youths were willing to make sacrifices to work in their kitchens. But there was little indication that the market for chefs operated in this way in the area covered by the present study. Restaurant workers were able to evaluate the quality of instruction in the kitchens where they had worked, but they did not possess broad knowledge of training opportunities. The expected wage differential was not present: learners and nonlearners received roughly the same pay for equivalent work.

Several factors appear to explain this anomaly. First, it is not clear that there is a net training cost to be transferred from the employer to the trainee. Much of the training process is free: opportunities for observation and practice are present in the job whether or not the incumbent takes advantage of them, and there is no added cost if he does so. The chef's efforts to aid the learning process, which might be expected to increase the cost of production, appear to depend largely on his personal style of operation. One of the respondents, for example, described a chef who was so secretive that he sent all of the kitchen help on fetch-and-

12 See Barbara la Fourtain's article on Master Chef Fessaquet in the *New York Times,* September 1, 1968.

carry errands before he made a sauce. The good instructors operate naturally and openly, talk about what they are doing as they work, and delegate responsibility readily. On the other hand, there is probably little the employer can do to expand or contract the amount of instruction that occurs, short of discharging the chef. Even so, it is not clear that the personal styles most conducive to training are inherently less productive than the styles that are not. And, in fact, given the relatively small size of the kitchen, the dominant position of the chef within it, and the close working relations between the chef and the manager (who is sometimes the owner as well), the amount of instruction provided subordinates is probably one of the lesser among the cost variables affected by the chef's personal traits.

An analogous argument can be made with respect to the subordinates whom the chef trains. Other things being equal, learners will be considerably more productive than nonlearners, since advancement in the restaurant industry requires motivation and drive. The difference in productivity may be enough, even more than enough, to compensate for the added cost of instruction.

At best, however, this line of reasoning will explain why employer efforts to escape the burden of training costs do not generate wage differentials. It does not explain the failure of competition for positions under good teaching chefs to produce differentials. Here, two other factors may be operative. First, it is possible that there are simply not enough individuals seeking instruction to create competition. A second explanation, not necessarily exclusive of the first, is that the information required to evaluate the merits of alternative positions is not readily available. Its paucity was suggested by the tendency of very enterprising individuals to speak of good learning positions as if their discovery were largely a matter of luck. Such an explanation becomes more likely when one considers the complexity of the information that existing channels must carry and the variety of negative job characteristics for which wage differentials must compensate. The quality of instruction is not the only factor that distinguishes one kitchen from another; there is also wide variation with respect to working hours, opportunities for overtime, the heat, the excitement of the job, and the pressure under which it is performed. Even instruction is not of a piece. Individuals do not generally acquire all of their skills in one kitchen: a given kitchen may be a good place to learn at one stage in a cook's development but not at another. Instruction, moreover, is to some extent individual, in the nature of a tutorial between the chef and his subordinate. It occurs in a kitchen at meal hour under great pressure and intense heat, and the personalities of the two may determine whether or not learning occurs. Thus, an efficient matching of students and teachers requires the circulation of an amount of information that any system would be hard pressed to provide.

In sum, then, the worker-programmed pattern that predominates in the training of restaurant cook-chefs is distinguished by (1) the motivation, initiative, and enterprise required of the individual worker; (2) the burden of direct costs for formal institutional instruction that it places on the trainee; and (3) the importance of the diffusion of information and of wage differentials in matching good teaching chefs with subordinates who will profit from exposure to them.

A strong argument can be made that at least in the labor market where the present study was conducted, these characteristics lead to an underinvestment in cooks' training relative to employer-sponsored training in other occupations. Evidence for underinvestment is the failure of the expected wage differentials to materialize. This failure implies *either* an absence of the information flows and the chef-subordinate matching required for efficient operation of the market *or* an excess training capacity within the industry, that is, more than enough teaching chefs to meet the demand of workers seeking instruction. The former points toward governmental intervention to facilitate information flows and improve the matching process. The latter is not in itself sufficient to warrant governmental intervention. The excess supply of teachers over students could result from real social costs that make cooks' training less desirable than training for other occupations. However, the motivational attributes and the resources required of would-be cooks but not of trainees in occupations where training is employer-sponsored give us reason to believe that some of the factors restraining the supply of cook trainees are the incidental result of market organization and would be overcome, at relatively little cost and with some net social benefit, by governmental intervention.

Current concern for the economic progress of disadvantaged and particularly black workers strengthens the argument for federal intervention. It is precisely these people who are least likely to possess the motivational traits required for progress in the restaurant industry. They are, however, disproportionately represented among restaurant cooks. The restaurant industry, moreover, has a tolerance for the instability of disadvantaged workers that is lacking in concentrated industries with well-developed internal labor markets. And the apparent shortage of cooks, combined with the high turnover and relative ease of upward mobility that high turnover implies, should make it possible for individuals to progress without appearing to threaten the position of those directly above them on the socio-economic ladder.

The cook-chef training program reviewed for this study consisted of two basic components: a ten-week period of full-time classroom instruction (during which the trainee received a stipend, which most trainees supplemented by part-time work before or after school), succeeded by forty weeks of training on the job. During the second phase, the class also met once a week in the evening for additional classroom instruction. The bridge between the classroom and on-the-job components, and in fact the pivot of the whole program, was the *trainer-coach*. The coach served as instructor in the classroom phase; he then solicited on-the-job training slots and placed individual trainees. The on-the-job instructor was provided largely by the enterprise's own chef, and participating restaurants were paid $12 a week per trainee to free the chef's time for this purpose. But the coach regularly visited the trainee on the job to supplement the chef's instruction and to counsel the trainee and occasionally his supervisor. When a trainee had exhausted the opportunities for instruction in one job, or when irreconcilable conflicts between the trainee and his supervisor arose, the trainer-coach found him a new position. In this way, the trainer-coach played the role of the employer in the employer-sponsored training pattern, acting as a substitute for the motivation and enterprise that would otherwise be required of the trainee. The coach also substituted for the role that wage differentials ought ideally to perform, chaneling information about potential trainees and instructors and insuring that the proper marriage between them occurred. Thus, the classroom portion of the program alleviated not only the burden of direct costs but also that of the worker's having to find such programs on his own in proprietary schools and community colleges, leaving the wage supplement paid to the employers as the only component of the program that does not appear to make sense in terms of the deficiencies of the industries' endogenous training patterns. As was seen earlier, wage differentials do not appear necessary to compensate for the cost of on-the-job instruction, nor do they occur. Most employers questioned on the subject seemed to feel the supplement was irrelevant. One manager reported that the supplement upset his accountants considerably. For a while, they insisted that he place it in escrow.

While the program appeared well designed and capable of overcoming the deficiencies of endogenous training patterns, it does not, however, necessarily follow that it succeeded in doing so. The services that the program offers are not only of value to workers who could not progress without them; they are also of value to people who would achieve training and advancement in the industry on their own. These people, moreover, precisely because they possess the motivation and enterprise required for success, will also be the most active in seeking out programs of this kind and pressing for admission. They have easy access to the trainer-coach, who by the nature of his work circulates widely in the local labor market. If the most highly motivated are not to capture the program, therefore, the coach must be prepared to resist this pressure and seek out instead the unaggressive disadvantaged workers who are not likely to apply on their own. It was clear in the restaurant programs—and in the tool and die program, which followed a very similar format—that the coach had not succeeded in screening out candidates capable of making it on their own. The most conspicuous failure in this regard occurred in the case of a chef in a large cafeteria who employed a second trainee as his assistant and who was avowedly interested in the program for the formal instruction it provided. Other less extreme cases could be cited.

Counterexamples of trainees who did not seem to have sufficient internal resources to succeed on their own (for whom success without the aid of the program is dubious) can be also cited, but whether on balance there are enough of these cases to outweigh the numbers on the other side and to justify the program is a moot question. It was initially thought that a control group could be used for this purpose, but it is under what would be a suitable type of control. Use of trainees in a nonsponsored program—the control group planned in the original project proposal—is simply not feasible; there is no such program. A random sample of the present population of chefs is one alternative, but since it does not appear possible for the industry to continue to draw as heavily on Europe for training as it has in the past, the current group of chefs will not reveal the character of those who will autonomously enter the occupation in the future. A random sample of restaurant workers from whom the supply of new chefs must be drawn appears to provide a better control. But it was apparent from interviewing the trainees that no obvious, easily measurable attributes could be used to distinguish those who would have made it on their own. The critical variable is enterprise and motivation, but the trainees whose enterprise and motivation were most apparent had the external characteristics that are associated with the lack of these traits, that is, race and parental background. Because neither of the investigators were psychologists, no finer psychological measures were attempted. Instead, a second fix upon the programs was tried: an examination of the institutional environment in which they operated and of the incentives present in the environment to orient the programs in the socially desirable direction.

Motivation of the Sponsoring Institutions

The preceding section suggests that the three training programs were under great pressure to support the endogenous training patterns of the occupations studied. It was clear that at least to some extent the programs succumbed to this pressure and simply took the place of training that would otherwise have been privately executed and financed. Whether the programs nonetheless made some net contribution to training is a moot question: it was not possible to answer it from the data gathered in the studies, and it is not clear exactly what kind of data would permit definitive judgments on this issue.

An alternative approach to this question is to examine the process through which the programs were funded and the motivation of the sponsoring institutions in order to identify the factors that are likely to lead them to resist (or accede to) pressures to conform to endogenous patterns and that are likely to impel them to extend the same amount of training provided by these patterns.

The offset printing program was dependent upon five institutions: the two sponsoring institutions, a trade-union local and a local trade association; a local employer who rented facilities for the program and from whose supervisory force the instructors were hired; and two government agencies, the Division of Employment Security and the Bureau of Apprenticeship Training, whose approval was required for funding. The catalyst in the program was the union, whose president was largely responsible for organizing it. He was avowedly motivated by concern for the fate of letterpress operators displaced by the introduction of offset printing, and this provided the rationale for the project. As noted earlier, however, there were very few displaced letterpress operators: the market for them was exceedingly tight, and it was probably for this reason that employers preferred to train new men for offset. A more plausible explanation for the union's interest, therefore, appeared to be the hope that by training its members and placing them in offset jobs it could establish a claim to jurisdiction over the whole of that process. Its claim to parts of the process, particularly plate making and stripping, was otherwise tenuous.

The union contacted the firm that provided the instructor and facilities through the regional graphic-arts institute. The firm was at the time converting some of its letterpress to offset, which was apparently what led the institute to recommend it to the union. The firm's management frankly admitted in interviews that it was attracted by the prospect of federal funding for training that the firm would otherwise have had to finance itself. Its one condition for participation was that it be given freedom to choose the people from the company to be admitted to the program. The idea of seeking MDTA funding—and in fact the whole of the program's format and content—derived from an earlier federally funded program run by another local of the international union in Oakland, California. The two proposals are almost identical. The fact that they were so similar greatly facilitated the task of obtaining approval from the required government agencies. These agencies relied heavily upon the precedent of the California programs in assessing the soundness of the curriculum and the budget. The program derived from the early phase of MDTA, when it was chiefly concerned with automation and structural unemployment: the fact that a technological change was involved was a controlling factor. A last requirement for approval was certification by the Division of Employment Security of the existence of a shortage of offset press operators.

In the tool and die program, the participating institutions included the trade association, which sponsored the program, the employers who hired the trainees during the on-the-job training phase, and, again, the Division of Employment Security and the Bureau of Apprenticeship Training. The central figure in the development of the program was a classic Schumpeterian entrepreneur (known in the trade as an operator). He originated the trainer-coach format, sold the idea to the regional tool and die association of which he was the executive director, and in his capacity as executive director hired his own consulting firm to set up and run the initial program of 20 trainees. The trade association, subcontracting through the consulting firm, afterward established tool and die training projects funded by MDTA in several cities in the region. The tool and die program included in the present study was one of these.

The entrepreneur who got the program started was obviously attracted by the federal funding. Some of the larger cooperating companies were also attracted by the idea of substituting federal funds for their own, although several smaller employers may have been induced to cooperate through a sense of duty to the craft and the industry. The eloquence of the trainer-coach on this subject was reflected in the comments of participating employers. Many of the smaller employers were also moved, however, by the recruiting services that the trainer-coach provided. The trade association was ostensibly motivated by the mutual interest of its members in overcoming the shortage of craftsmen, but it was also apparent that the program became a justification for an organization whose raison d'être was otherwise questionable. Approval by the government agencies was greatly facilitated by the fact that they were presented with a standard format that they had previously endorsed. Indeed, there is a sense in which previous endorsements made it impossible to refuse a request to extend the program. Such a refusal would have called into question the judgment of colleagues and superiors responsible for funding earlier programs, and the officials making such decisions were not in a position to collect the evidence necessary to sustain such an action.

The cook-chef program was developed by the same entrepreneur who promoted the tool and die program, probably in an attempt to extend his range of operations by capitalizing on the tool and die experience. The restaurant association, which nominally sponsored the tool and die program, was organized by the entrepreneur for this purpose. (It subsequently branched out to the training of waitresses.) The association hired the entrepreneur as its executive director and subcontracted the training to the entrepreneur's firm. Like the tool and die program, the cooks' training program included in this study was one of several regional offshoots of a project begun on a very small scale in the entrepreneur's home town. In his restaurant activities, the entrepreneur made use of his contacts within the U.S. Department of Labor and of the extensive knowledge about how to promote training programs there that he had acquired in connection with the tool and die program. His restaurant activities also benefited from experience gathered in the tool and die industry with training in general and with the use of the trainer-coach format in a dispersed employment industry in particular. For the government agencies involved, familiarity with the training format and with the personnel of the sponsoring organization facilitated the approval of the initial contract, which in turn led to the approval of subsequent programs. For the government and for the promoter, a cooks' program had the additional advantage of operating in an industry that employed large numbers of minority group members at a time when federal officials were placing increasing emphasis on this goal. The restaurateurs were attracted to the program (and to the association) by the recruiting services of the trainer-coach.

The preceding synopsis makes it clear that the individuals and the nongovernmental institutions participating in the training programs under study had no intrinsic interest in resisting pressure to support the endogenous training patterns; some in fact were themselves the source of such pressure. Under these circumstances, resistance, if there is to be any, must be generated by the federal agencies through the process of funding and review.

The federal agencies in the present instance failed to generate such pressure. Their attention was confined to the certification of a shortage in the occupation for which training was provided and a review of the training procedures and concomitant costs. No attempts were made to insure that the training would actually serve to supplement endogenous patterns and not merely substitute for them. A partial exception was the emphasis on recruitment of the disadvantaged in reviewing proposals, which appears to have affected at least the orientation of the restaurant program. Unfortunately, the criterion "disadvantaged"—or the group of variables used to define it—was not sensitive enough to distinguish between those whose progress in the industry required the assistance of a special program and those with the motivation and drive required to advance on their own. The latter were not, therefore, effectively screened out.

The generation of resistance to pressure to conform to existing training patterns is not solely a question of intent. A set of criteria with the capacity of distinguishing, either for purposes of program design and administration or for assessment of the results of a completed project, institutions and individuals who would not have become engaged in training autonomously is not obvious. The straightforward approach is to ask participating individuals if the program affects their basic training decision and exclude those who say no, but clearly this approach creates a tremendous incentive for people to lie. The fact that several firms in the present study answered negatively is probably less a sign of their intrinsic honesty than of the absence of pressure within the program to avoid the windfall that an affirmative answer implies.

Without the cooperation of the individuals involved, a more elaborate test is required to screen out those who would have trained on their own, some kind of psychological and motivational test for the labor force in occupations where training is worker-programmed, an elaborate typology for firms in industries where employer-sponsored training prevails. It is possible that psychologists have developed instruments capable of making the required distinctions among individuals, but economists have no instruments to make the required distinctions among firms.

A partial substitute for the explicit objective tests of the social scientist is the "smell" test of a person who has grown up in the industry. Those who really know a given industry seem to be able to tell when people within it are being moved to depart from established practice and procedure. Such judgments are not neat and clear; the reasoning that underlies them cannot always be verbalized, and even where the reasoning is explicit the evidence required to support it can seldom be mustered. An agency accountable to the public has a limited capacity to base its decisions upon criteria of this kind. Nevertheless, the capacity that it does have might be sufficient to apply the needed pressure on the programs. A policy of this kind requires at least one expert on the agency staff for each industry involved in training: a good sense of "smell" in more than one industry is a very rare attribute.

Elaborate tests involving large, specialized staffs are, however, deterred by the procedure through which the programs are funded. Projects of less than $50,000 are approved through the local office of the Bureau of Apprenticeship and Training without regional or national review. Each of the projects studied fell below this ceiling. The printing program costs roughly $15,000, the tool and die project about $20,000, the cooks project about $35,000. Thus the cost of prefunding investigation quickly escalates toward the cost of the project, and elaborate procedures cannot be justified. The local office, quite rightly from its perspective, relies upon a cursory review and places great weight on the precedent of similar contracts funded elsewhere, which serves as a cheap proxy for more expensive measures for achieving program soundness. Post-project evaluations are also deterred. The local office tends to view projects as isolated instances that do not survive to benefit from whatever evaluations might uncover. In fact, however, many of the projects are not isolated instances but part of a national network that, in the case of the offset press program, included at least one other project and, in the tool and die and cooks' cases, a large number. At least 19 cooks' projects, for example, had been *completed* before the project in this study was begun. Moreover, all three programs studied were repeated several times at the same sites, and for the pressmen and tool and die programs each repetition involved a separate contract. Only for the cooks' training was the series of projects eventually consolidated in a single large regional contract that attracted national attention and justified an elaborate investigation, and by the time it was consolidated the number of separately funded projects in this industry and in tool and die may have been sufficient to deter really dispassionate review. Thus, even if it were feasible to develop criteria that effectively distinguished new training opportunities, it is not clear that existing review procedures could make use of them.

Finally, there remains the question of whether, assuming criteria that would distinguish individuals and institutions who would engage in training on their own and an administrative procedure that could apply the criteria so as to exclude them, the nongovernmental institutions now participating in the program would continue to participate. In the cooks' and tool and die programs—or, to put it more broadly, in those occupations where training is worker-programmed and the program utilizes a trainer-coach—continued participation appears likely. For the entrepreneur who organized these programs the attraction was partly the excitement of the game, partly the game's reward. Under the new rules, both would remain. In fact, the recruiting services of the trainer-coach which attracted employer participation would also remain. Training as a raison d'être for the trade association would continue as well, although the trade association appears important chiefly as a vehicle for the entrepreneur, and one would think a clever entrepreneur could find substitutes for it.

4

Union Policies toward the Admission of Apprentices

George Strauss

Apprenticeship has been the butt of much criticism, both from civil rights groups and from manpower experts. Among the major criticisms have been that the unions that control apprenticeship restrict entry excessively, which creates monopolies, manpower shortages, and excessively high wage rates, and that they engage in favoritism, discriminating against blacks and in favor of relatives and friends of members.

This is a brief report on union policies toward admission, based on interviews and obeservations in northern California and to a lesser extent in western New York. The study was confined primarily to the building trades and dealt chiefly with the period 1962–1966.[1] All these limitations deserve further comment.

1. The geographical limitation may be least serious. Other studies[2] (and my own interviews) suggest that the

1 The research was conducted under a Ford Foundation grant to the Institute of Industrial Relations, University of California, Berkeley, for research on unemployment and the American economy. The field work included interviews with apprentices, business agents, management representatives, Joint Apprenticeship Committee and governmental coordinators, as well as observation of JAC and union meetings, for a total of over 190 interviews and over 100 meetings and classes.

2 See, for example, Howard Brighton, "Apprentice Selection Practices of the Building Construction Trade Unions in Oklahoma" (Ph.D. thesis, University of Oklahoma, 1965); Karl Magnusen, "A Study of Registered Joint Apprenticeship Committees in Wisconsin Building Trades" (Ed.D. thesis, University of Wisconsin, 1964); *Building Trades: Analysis of Apprenticeship Selection Standards in the New York City Area* (New York: New York State Commission for Human Rights, 1968). References to the specific geographical areas covered in these works will not be noted further.

situation in the areas studied is roughly typical of the rest of the country, though some exceptions will be noted later.

2. Registered apprenticeship is concentrated in the building, printing, and metal (chiefly machinist) trades. In these trades, and particularly in the building trades, apprenticeship is largely controlled by union-dominated Joint Apprenticeship Committees (JACs), which operate on an areawide, multifirm basis. Apprenticeship in mass production industries (auto, steel, and so on) is subject to very different admission practices, and the union plays a somewhat less important role in them. My comments apply only to areawide, JAC-controlled programs, and primarily to the building trades.

3. The period 1963–1966 was one of increasing formalization and centralization of admission practices, in part as a reaction to growing civil rights pressures, but also for other reasons to be discussed. While this process has continued since then, its main outlines were observable at the time this study was carried out.

The Role of Apprenticeship

In theory, apprenticeship is the principle means of entry into the crafts. In fact, only a minority of craftsmen receive full apprenticeship training.[3] A majority have picked up their skills through informal training, often in nonunion, rural, or industrial jobs, and they are directly admitted to the union without formal apprenticeship. Indeed, the

[3] For further discussion, see George Strauss, "Apprenticeship: An Evaluation of the Need," in *Employment Policy and the Labor Market,* ed. Arthur M. Ross (Berkeley: University of California Press, 1965).

function of apprenticeship today seems largely to be that of training skilled keymen, and the proportion of job entrants provided by each trade's apprenticeship program seems to be related to the skill mix that the trade requires. Employers seem to have adjusted to the use of a substantial proportion of semiskilled men.

Thus apprenticeship is at most only a partially effective barrier to entry into the trade. To be sure, restrictions on the number of apprentices may have short-term effect during periods of slack work when other means of entry are also closed, but over the long run they may lead to more extensive use of other channels.

The Range of Admission Procedures

Procedures for admission to unions are diverse. The effective "gatekeeper" may be the employer, the business agent, the JAC, the vocational school instructor, or a government consultant. The programs may be simple or elaborate. Preferential treatment for relatives and friends may be the rule, or objective standards may prevail. The following are examples of the range I found in practice:[4]

Union A Employers do the hiring. No JAC approval required. Union plays a negligible role in finding an applicant a job.

Union B Applicant must find job first, then get JAC approval, but can work until its ruling is made. Few applicants

[4] Names of individual unions cannot be revealed because the data were collected under a pledge that they would be kept confidential. Antidiscrimination regulations now require unions to make their selection procedures public; however, formally announced procedures often deviate from those followed in practice.

rejected by JAC. Most apprentices are friends or relatives of contractors or members.

Union C No apprentices admitted in winter. At other times applicants must appear before JAC, which screens them to make sure they meet minimum requirements. Tightness of screening varies with the business cycle. Approved applicants placed on waiting list but in practice must find job on their own.

Union D During peak construction, when all qualified journeymen are at work, employers are free to hire nonmembers on permit. Apprentices are then selected from permit men, presumably on the basis of ability shown on the job.

Union E This local has set a maximum size for itself. Apprentices admitted only when membership falls below maximum. Though the union contract calls for a JAC, in practice the decision is made by the business agent. Most apprentices are sons.

Union F Applicants must take extensive examinations given by the local community college and then appear before JAC, where they are interviewed at length. Each applicant is rated by each JAC member on a printed form. Sons are admitted if they do moderately well. The remaining vacancies are filled on the basis of interview and test scores.

Union G An applicant who scores above the thirtieth percentile in an examination given by the local high school must appear before the JAC for an interview. Once past this hurdle, he is placed on a waiting list. If still interested after a wait of up to eighteen months, he is sent to a full-time preapprenticeship school run by the union. After three months in school, he appears before a five-man committee, which gives him a practical project taking six hours to complete. If he passes this test and has done well in class, he is formally admitted to the program. Until actually sent out on a job, he must continue in school for as long as six months more.

The trend in recent years has been toward more formal and objective procedures, with greater authority concentrated in the JACs. This tendency is especially apparent in the higher-status trades,[5] such as electricians, plumbers, and sheet-metal workers, and in certain areas of the country, such as California and New York.

The Size of Apprenticeship Programs

Unions usually control the size of apprenticeship programs either by setting ratios of apprentices to journeymen for the individual employer or by setting quotas for the trade as a whole.[6] Traditionally, ratio rules were the most important restrictive device, but today, as selection procedures become more formalized and centralized, quotas seem to have assumed greater significance, particularly in the higher-status trades.

5 For measures of status, see Strauss, "Apprenticeship," p. 308.

6 Though some forms of apprenticeship regulations are imposed unilaterally by the union (as in Union E), in most cases these regulations are at least technically the product of collectively bargained JAC decisions. Generally, apprenticeship is a matter of greater concern to unions than to management, and, at least in the construction trade, management normally goes along with union wishes without raising much objection. Management in manufacturing has somewhat greater freedom both to determine the size of the program and to select individual apprentices.

Other regulatory techniques are also used.[7] Requirements of long apprenticeships limit the number of apprentices who become journeymen in any one year. If wage rates are excessively high, this may discourage employers from hiring apprentices. Age and education limitations may reduce the number of applicants. Though ratio and quota limitations are the most important restrictions, many unions employ combinations of all the methods described.

Ratios Where ratio rules are the primary form of restriction (as they were in Unions A, B, C, and D), the prospective apprentice finds his job essentially by himself. The JAC activity is limited either to giving him a "hunting license" or to granting him an indenture after he has found an employer willing to take him on. The JAC evaluation of the apprentice's merits in these cases is often fairly perfunctory (for example, as in Union B); the real choice among applicants is made by the individual employer (subject, of course, to general restrictions as to age, education, and so forth).

Ratio rules have been subject to considerable debate. They have often been blamed for the low number of apprentices trained. The standard answer to these charges is that "employers, with rare exceptions, hire fewer than the rules permit."[8] Certainly statistics as to the number of appren-

[7] Simon Rottenberg argues on classical economic grounds that any restriction of the free competitive process, either in terms of setting wages or of fixing an arbitrary length for apprenticeship, operates to restrict entry. The union restricts entry whenever it "specifies the terms of employment for apprentices [rather than] leaves them to be determined by the market." "The Irrelevance of Union Apprenticeship/Journeymen Ratios," *Journal of Business* 34 (July 1961): 384–386.

[8] Sumner Slichter, *Union Policies and Industrial Management* (Washington, D.C.: Brookings Institution, 1941), p. 28.

tices employed nationwide seem to bear this out. In most trades the *actual* ratio of apprentices to journeymen employed is 1:10 or 1:20, far lower than ratio rules typically permit. Yet these data may be somewhat misleading, since ratio limitations are applied not on a nationwide basis but employer by employer. Even though many employers take no apprentices at all, others hire all their ratio permits and might like to hire more. In addition, some unions place flat limitations on the number of apprentices that any firm may hire, regardless of its size.

In one situation observed (in the printing industry), ratio rules clearly reduced the number of apprentices significantly. In other situations, a small but not insignificant number of employers hired the maximum number of apprentices the rules allowed and might have hired more. In practice, however, the rules were less restrictive than they might have been because they were waived in times of full employment for employers who did a good job in training. In northern California ratios did not seem greatly restrictive and were less so than quotas. The picture may be different elsewhere.[9]

Quotas With the quota system, the JAC determines the size of the program, either explicitly, through fixing a quota of apprentices to be admitted during a given period (as occurred in Unions F and G), or implicitly, through alter-

[9] According to a 1966 survey of the building trades in Wisconsin, 30 out of 101 JACs responding reported that they had an "excess of apprenticeship applicants" because "apprentice-journeymen ratio filled"; the 30 included 8 out of the 13 electrical JACs. On the other hand, 8 of these electrical committees reported that most "employers had fewer apprentices than ratio allowed." Magnusen, "A Study of Registered Joint Apprenticeship Committees," pp. 143, 134.

nately "opening the books" to new apprentices and then closing them when enough are hired (as occurred in Union E). In this case, application is made directly to the JAC, which fills the quota from among those who have applied for admission. Once an applicant is approved, his name is placed on a list, and he is dispatched by the union business agent (or JAC coordinator or secretary) when a qualified employer requests an apprentice. This system does not guarantee an apprentice a job, since the employer does the actual hiring, but the applicant's chances of being put to work are very good because committees try not to approve more applicants than the market can absorb. Ratio rules may still apply to individual firms, but the overall quota is the primary form of regulation.

Overconservative estimates The quota system provides more flexibility than the ratio system because unions set quotas generally on the basis of their estimate of the market's ability to absorb apprentices without causing unemployment, while ratios are rarely changed from year to year.[10] A number of factors, however, tend to make union estimates at least slightly overconservative. Shortsighted as it may be, there are strong political pressures within the union to curtail admission whenever there is unemployment, regardless of long-run prospects. A new group of apprentices is not likely to be admitted if some members of the previous group are still unplaced. Even if all apprentices are placed, a union is reluctant to admit additional ones if there are journeymen out of work. On the other hand, if all present members are at work but long-run prospects seem poor, business agents

10 Although, as has been seen, ratios are sometimes suspended in times of high employment.

will be under pressure to meet current shortages by taking in members on a temporary permit or transfer basis, rather than by increasing the size of the permanent work force through apprenticeship. Thus there is pressure to reduce the size of apprenticeship programs whenever *either* the short- or long-term employment prospects for *either* apprentices or journeymen begin to cloud up.

From the union's point of view, there are many short-run advantages to admitting men to the labor market through the "back door" rather than through apprenticeship. Apprenticeship involves a guess as to the future, and many unions fear to expand their apprenticeship program too fast, not knowing what business conditions may be three to five years hence when the apprentices complete their training. Men admitted through the back door are already partly trained, and they enter the labor market only during the busy season when all regular members are working. Many come in on a permit that can be revoked when times get worse. In many instances, the only way to organize a nonunion firm is through taking its employees into the union.

Another reason for the unions' conservatism is the fact that union members who favor restriction are generally more vocal than those who are opposed. The restrictionists generally come from what is sometimes called the "mourners' bench," older or poorly trained members who find it difficult to obtain work and who tend to look upon newly admitted apprentices as the cause of their troubles. Such members are more likely to attend union meetings than members who find work easily, and they use the meetings as a forum for their grievances.

On the whole, therefore, union officials prefer to play it

safe and err on the side of keeping admissions low. It is more dangerous to have too many members than too few. If estimates turn out too low, overtime and direct admission can handle the labor shortage. But if estimates are too high, the business agent will be plagued with members out of work. As a consequence, admission to apprenticeship is often suspended whenever jobs are scarce. Thus the intake into programs is erratic, and their size tends to be flexible downward but rather rigid upward. It is fairly easy to reduce the number of apprentices admitted but politically difficult to raise it. Nevertheless, except in times of peak employment, most locals usually have at least a few unemployed apprentices on the bench, which suggests that apprentice supply is reasonably well matched to demand.[11] Fundamentally, employer willingness to hire is a basic determinant of the size of apprenticeship programs. Therefore, we must look briefly at apprenticeship from the employer's point of view.

Employer's point of view Statistics as to the extent to which employers participate in apprenticeship are quite limited. However, it seems clear that considerably less than half the construction firms eligible take part in apprenticeship and that very few of these take as many apprentices as their ratio permits. Participation is even less in manufacturing. Why should apprenticeship be so unattractive to employers?

[11] True, without quotas a larger number of new apprentices might be taken on during peak periods, thus reducing the number of back-door entrants. On the other hand, from the employer's point of view peak employment is not the time to start a completely green hand.

From a purely economic point of view, the chief reason that an employer hires apprentices is his hope that after training they will stay on as skilled journeymen. In addition, it is argued that apprentices, as a cheap form of labor, pay for themselves even during training.

Employers generally agree that journeymen who have been trained as apprentices make better employees than those who have not. However, high rates of turnover are quite discouraging. According to California studies, about half the apprentices change employers during apprenticeship and 70 percent do so during their first five years as journeymen, with turnover being higher in construction than in manufacturing. With turnover figures as high as this, many employers pirate journeymen from others rather than training their own.

The costs and benefits to the employer of an apprentice during his training period are difficult to measure.[12] Though beginning apprentices earn only about half the journeyman's rate, their productivity may be a great deal less. Wages are not the only cost of apprenticeship. An apprentice must receive training from someone, usually a journeyman or foreman. Both instructor and apprentice lose time from work while instruction is going on. In some areas (notably Wisconsin) employers are expected to pay their apprentices while they take classroom instruction, usually for four hours a week. Apprenticeship programs require considerable paperwork, reports to JACs

[12] A few studies have attempted to measure costs, but it is difficult to generalize from them. I suspect that costs will vary greatly and will depend among other things on the thoroughness of the training offered.

and government agencies, training schedules, and so forth. In addition, apprenticeship may cause difficulty in scheduling work. In assigning men to jobs, the conscientious foreman must consider not only who is best for the job but also the apprentice's training needs. Having a considerable number of partially trained apprentices may reduce the flexibility of the work force.

All in all, the expenses of training apprentices are quite substantial. How about the returns in terms of productivity? Some employers claim that an apprentice does not begin to pay his way until his second or third year and that only in the fourth year does the employer make any "profit" from him. Indeed, a major argument for long apprenticeship is that unless employers can make money on fourth-year apprentices they will not hire first-year ones.

Actually an employer can make money from an apprentice rather quickly if he assigns him to simple, routine tasks. (Thus, an electrical contractor specializing in tract houses can put an apprentice to work doing simple wiring. In a short time, he can develop proficiency and fairly soon work every bit as fast as a trained journeyman.) But what is in the contractor's interest is of course not in the interest of the apprentice. The whole apprenticeship training scheme assumes that the apprentice receives a well-rounded education in all phases of the work. To get maximum training efficiency, as soon as the apprentice learns one operation, he should be transferred to another. Obviously, this is expensive to the employer; the more rapid the rotation among jobs, the more the apprentice learns from his training, but the greater the immediate cost to the employer.

This creates a dilemma for the union and for the JAC. On one hand, they have a justified fear that unless rotation is enforced, employers will use apprenticeship as a source of cheap labor and apprentices will learn relatively little. On the other hand, if they enforce rotation too strictly, they may reduce or eliminate the incentive for employers to take on apprentices at all.

Apprenticeship with its significant externalities provides a classic case for Becker's analysis.[13] Broad training, which is advantageous to employers as a group, is somewhat less advantageous to the individual employer. Thus employers have an incentive either to provide only a narrow apprenticeship or to take on Joe McGees (unskilled men) who can be trained very quickly on the job.

Why Does Apprenticeship Continue?

Given the various factors that tend to depress the size of apprenticeship, perhaps the real question is why apprenticeship continues at all. Part of the explanation is that the principle of apprenticeship has had steady union support. There are three reasons for this support:

1. Many union members look upon apprenticeship as a means of controlling entry into the trade, and as the sole means of subjecting the acquisition of skills to direct union control (as compared with vocational schooling, for example). This viewpoint tends to exaggerate the importance of apprenticeship, however. Were the crafts able to out-

[13] Gary S. Becker, *Human Capital* (New York: National Bureau of Economic Research, 1964). See also Lester Thurow, "The Role of Manpower Policy in Achieving Aggregate Goals," in *Toward a Manpower Policy,* ed. Robert A. Gordon (New York: John Wiley & Sons, 1967).

law all forms of training other than apprenticeship, or even if all jobs demanded the full range of journeyman skills (which presumably could be acquired only through apprenticeship), then apprenticeship might well be an effective means of control. In fact, neither of these conditions obtains, and as a consequence there is a substantial amount of back-door entry. Regardless, the myth persists that the existence of apprenticeship permits the union to maintain tighter control over the labor market.

2. Even those who do not look upon apprenticeship as a means of restricting numbers do see it as a means of acquiring skills. Business agents almost universally agree that from a long-run point of view back-door admissions are unwise and should be discouraged. The union's ability to control its jurisdiction depends in part on the skill of its members: if the business agent is not able to send competent men to the employer, the employer may be tempted to work on a nonunion basis. Furthermore, the presence of unskilled men in the union makes the business agent's life more difficult; unskilled men are harder to place; they are far more likely than skilled men to insist on various types of featherbedding to preserve their jobs; and internal schisms develop in the union as the unskilled insist that jobs be shared equally. "Almost all my troubles I get from poorly trained mechanics," a business agent commented, and his was a typical view.

3. Finally, poorly trained men threaten the craft's sense of pride and identification. A well-run apprenticeship program is a sign of craft status. Having higher-skilled men (and the existence of an apprenticeship program to pro-

vide them) helps legitimate the union's right to wage increases.

These factors help explain why most craft unions have a strong formal commitment to apprenticeship as a preferred source of supply, even though in practice they may take the bulk of their members through back-door channels. Thus, business agents do exert a certain amount of informal pressure (which varies according to the circumstances) on employers to take on apprentices. As one business agent put it, "Every time an employer asks for four or more journeymen, I ask him to take an apprentice too. With a little arm twisting I find I can get a lot of apprentices placed." Attitudes like this help overcome employer reluctance.

Support for apprenticeship cannot be explained on economic grounds alone. A high percentage of craft employers (or key members of management in large firms) are former craftsmen. They are fiercely proud of their craft and their industry and anxious to maintain its status. Indeed, business agents, contractors, superintendents, and foremen are, for the most part, ex-apprentices themselves. As old grads, they want to support their alma mater.

Decision Making in Practice: Union H

An illustration of the problems just mentioned is provided by the following case study of how a higher-status JAC made its decision in March on how many to admit to its next class in June.

At the time of this study, the trade had approximately 850 journeymen, 128 apprentices, and a 1:3 ratio rule.

About 50 of the 67 local contractors hired apprentices, a high proportion. With a four-year program, theoretically 20 new apprentices were started each June and December.

Employment conditions had been generally excellent over the preceding few years; however, fearing a long-term surplus of men, the local had curtailed back-door entry to the extent that the number of journeymen members (not those on permit) had declined slightly. A mild recession had occurred in the previous fall; some apprentices accepted in June did not find employment until December. Since December employment had been excellent, but almost entirely owing to one big project which was currently employing 250 craftsmen.

At the first meeting to consider the size of the new class, the JAC coordinator reported that 212 formal applications had been received (plus a number of informal inquiries). Ninety applicants met the age and education requirements and almost 70 had passed their tests. Of these, 6 were sons. The coordinator reported that he was finding it harder to place apprentices, and estimated he could take care of 15, but not 20.

The discussion lasted over three JAC meetings and spilled over into the union meeting. No one supported a full class of 20. Some argued in favor of admitting 15; others preferred 5 or none at all. The main arguments for the large class were: (1) all apprentices were working and apparently enough jobs could be found; and (2) "If we are going to keep this a skilled trade, we have got to keep these classes just as high as we can, even in bad times."

For the small class it was argued: (1) the big project would soon lay off 250 men and there was nothing comparable coming in to replace it. ("Perhaps it would be better to let the dust settle for a while. . . . Better a small class than lots of men out of work"); (2) men were hard to place last year; (3) because of worsening economic conditions, it was difficult to adhere to the JAC's program of rotating men from job to job at regular intervals.

Still another argument was that almost two-thirds of the apprentices were doing "tract work." While this provided good initial training, ideally apprentices should spend most of their time in industrial and commercial fields "where you can really learn something." The business agent commented that he had recently "yanked" two men off jobs where they were doing routine work without supervision. He could do this a lot more often if he "had some jobs up my sleeve where I could place them."

Discussion returned to the 250 men soon to be laid off. The business agent closed the debate: "Eleven apprentices are going to graduate in June but that doesn't mean there are going to be eleven more jobs in the industry. These men will be journeymen. The total number of men in the industry, apprentices plus journeymen, is what counts, not just the number in apprenticeship." The final decision, made several months later, was to accept 10 men with another 10 to go on the alternate list.

Postscript: These 10 were hard to place. The next class was eliminated altogether, and the size of the target class was reduced from 20 to 15. The following class had 10, and the one after that 15.

Selection Policies

In addition to deciding how many apprentices to admit, JACs that practice central selection must also decide which among the available candidates should be admitted. Until recently this was done on a highly informal basis: the JAC (or perhaps a union committee or even the business agent alone, as in Union E) would make the choice on the basis of their personal impressions of the candidates (subject to the heavy influence of political pressures). In recent years this process has been formalized and made to seem more impersonal and objective. The typical selection procedure today involves (1) meeting certain minimum standards, (2) taking a test, and (3) appearing for an interview before the JAC, after which (4) the JAC makes its selection.

Minimum Requirements

High school graduation is required by a substantial number of programs today,[14] for example in programs enrolling 80 per cent of the apprentices in Alameda and Contra Costa counties, California (as of June 1965), and in 35 out of 57 of the building trades programs in Metropolitan New York City (as of 1968).[15] The electricians and plumbers frequently require, in addition to high school, certain specific courses in mathematics.

The typical trade sets 18 as the minimum age of entry. Maximum ages vary widely, from 21 to over 30, with a median maximum age, both in New York City and in northern California, of 25. (Exceptions normally are made in the case of veterans.) In practice the average age of entry is 20 or 21, about two or three years out of high school.[16]

[14] American practice contrasts sharply with that in Europe. In most European countries, apprenticeship is looked upon as a substitute for high school. The most recent studies from various parts of the United States (dating from 1955 on) suggests that at least three-quarters of all apprentices are high school graduates and that about one-sixth have had some college (or other postsecondary school) experience. Similar developments have occurred among craftsmen generally. By 1967, the median years of school completed by craftsmen and foremen was 12.0, up from 9.7 in 1948.

[15] Exceptions are often made for those who have passed a high school equivalency exam (although, in one case observed, a high school drop-out was assumed to have absorbed the "equivalent of high school" through learning the trade from his father).

[16] Again American practice differs greatly from European, in which apprentices typically begin their training at age 14 or 15. Age 16 or 17 was common in this country before World War II. Our present relatively high age of entry is a carry-over from the immediate postwar G.I. Bill period when the government subsidized participation by veterans in apprenticeship. For a while the average age of entry was as high as 24.

Both education and age requirements have been tightened somewhat in recent years. As might be expected, it is the higher-status trades (electricians, plumbers, and sheet-metal workers) that have the tightest standards.

Many trades have additional requirements, such as a driver's license, a license to operate power-actuated tools, a physical examination, or freedom from color blindness (for electricians, who work with color-coded electric wires). A majority of the New York City construction programs require at least one year's residency in the New York area; many require three years or more. A substantial minority of the New York locals also disqualify those with police records or other than honorable discharges.

The establishment of minimum standards greatly reduces the number of applicants, making the JACs' task easier. Thus a high school graduation requirement and a $5 application fee reduced one trade's applicants by one-half.

Tests

In contrast to the situation twenty years ago, most trades now require applicants to take written tests. Recent studies from Oklahoma, Wisconsin, and Metropolitan New York City, plus our own from Alameda and Contra Costa counties, all indicate that over two-thirds of the programs require tests. As with other requirements, tests were adopted by the higher-status trades first, but the process has been hastened by antidiscrimination regulations requiring "objectivity." Thus, in the East Bay area, among the first trades to use tests were the electricians, plumbers, and machinists, and a similar process seems to have occurred elsewhere.

A wide variety of tests is used. Perhaps most common are those measuring general intelligence and numerical and verbal aptitude, followed by those measuring various forms of mechanical aptitude. The tests are subject to a number of criticisms.

1. My impression, based on observation, is that tests are often adopted without any attempt to validate their usefulness in a given situation, often merely because the title of the test seems appropriate or because a school official who has used the test for some other purpose has recommended it. JAC members have little understanding of what the various tests seek to measure or what test results mean. (In this unsophisticated attitude the construction industry is not much different from other branches of business, where tests are adopted with little understanding of their limitations.)

2. Most of the tests have been designed for purposes other than apprenticeship.[17] Thus, one of the most popular tests used in northern California, the School and College Test (SCAT), was developed to predict scholastic success. The Minnesota Multiphasic Inventory (reported in use by one JAC) is useful chiefly in detecting mental abnormalities.

3. Some of the few validation studies have been crude. Take, for example, the General Aptitude Test Battery (GATB), developed by the U.S. Employment Service and used extensively in some areas for apprentice selection.[18]

[17] Some progress has been made here. Several of the trades, especially the Operating Engineers, have retained consulting firms to develop tests especially suited to their needs .

[18] *Guide to the General Aptitude Test Battery,* U.S. Department of Labor, Bureau of Employment Security, Part II, Norms (Washington,

As far as the apprenticeable trades are concerned, this battery was validated with general small and noncomparable samples and with a tremendous range of criterion variables. A scrutiny of the methodology does not inspire confidence, and the final result of this mixed bag of studies, as expressed in cutting scores, is somewhat incongruous. For example, bricklayers require *more* numerical aptitude but *less* manual dexterity than any other construction trade in which numerical aptitude and mechanical dexterity are predictive factors.

4. The tests are primarily of the paper and pencil variety; only a few (among others, the GATB) measure manual ability. As a consequence, the training received by those who have gone to vocational high schools gives them relatively little advantage over those who have gone to academic high schools; indeed the reverse may be true, since the achievement tests most commonly given measure ability in reading and mathematics, subjects most intensively studied in academic high schools.

5. Normally, if the applicant fails a test, he is allowed to take it again. In some trades the same test is used over and over. In practice, this may lead to "leaks." Furthermore, scores usually improve the second time a test is taken, even if real ability remains unchanged. (The fact that test questions are predictable, if not directly, at least in terms of their general nature, helps explain the success of the "cram schools" that have been set up to help black applicants.)

D.C., January 1962) and Part III, Development (Washington, D.C., October 1962). I am well aware of the tremendous difficulties involved in developing and maintaining the GATB.

Tests and minorities Many tests used for selection purposes have been attacked for having built-in biases against blacks, and apprenticeship tests are no exception. In addition to the reasons listed earlier, it is argued that tests are "culturally biased," in that they have been developed in a white middle-class context and give undue weight, for example, to middle-class vocabulary. It is also argued that compared to black applicants from underprivileged areas, white applicants are more likely to have had extensive experience taking tests and to be comfortable in a test-taking situation.

A cause célèbre involved a series of tests given by court order to applicants for the New York City sheet-metal apprenticeship program. These tests, which were given by the New York University Testing and Advisory Center, were attacked by the noted black psychologist, Kenneth B. Clark, after the highest-ranking of 50 minority applicants came in sixty-eighth out of 340 taking the test. These tests sought to measure mental alertness, mechanical reasoning, space relations, and mathematical concepts. Professor Clark objected to these tests on three grounds:[19] (1) They were too hard. Though supposedly designed for the tenth-grade level, they were actually much more difficult. (2) They dealt with factors that were not relevant to sheet-metal apprenticeship. And (3) they emphasized skills, such as reading comprehension, that blacks in "criminally inferior . . . de facto segregated" schools are not properly taught.

The case has its ironic side. Extensive tutoring efforts conducted by the Workers Defense League were so success-

19 *New York Times,* April 13, 1965.

ful that within eighteen months, of the top 10 scorers on the test given by this same agency, 9 were black.[20] This time it was the union that sought to have the results set aside.

Interviews

Many trades, particularly the higher-status ones, require all applicants to appear for an interview or oral examination before the entire JAC. Interviews permit the JAC to keep some "control" over the selection process and prevent it from being purely "mechanistic" or "objective" (to use two contrasting value-loaded terms).

The length of these interviews varies, depending on the number of applicants. Typically, ten minutes are allowed. (Even so, if there is a large number of applicants, interviewing can be a heavy burden for JAC members.) An attempt is made to keep the proceedings friendly and informal; most JAC members are aware that questioning before a committee can be a frightening experience for a youth. Inevitably, however, applicants who already know members of the committee will feel more relaxed than those facing a group of complete strangers.

Of course there is no such thing as a typical interview, but in the cases observed the questions asked by the committee were often like this:

> Mr. Fitch, won't you sit down? Do you know the members of the committee? Allen Higgins from the union, Burt Newfane from the contractors' association. . . .
>
> Now (glancing at the application form) I gather you are 22? And you graduated from Falcolner High? What course

[20] *New York Times,* December 29, 1966.

did you take? Did you have any shop work? Did you like it? What kinds of grades did you get?

Then you were in the Army for two years. Did you do any-of our [craft's] work there? What kind?

After you got out of the Army you had several jobs. Would you tell the committee about them? Why did you quit your first job? When did you first think of becoming [a tradesman]? Did you ever talk it over with your father? What makes you think you'll make a good [tradesman]? Did you ever work [with our tools]?

You're married aren't you? Do you know that apprentices start at $—— and, though we try, we can't guarantee continuous employment? You may be out of work for considerable periods during the winter. You know that, don't you?

We require all apprentices to go to school two nights a week. Do you know that with all your school work and your regular job you won't be home much? What does your wife think of that?

Anyone else have any questions? Well, Mr. Finch, thank you for coming in. We'll write you a letter with our decision, but don't expect it for another four weeks.

Upon completion of the interview, it is common for each committee member to fill out a rating form (New York regulations require this). Normally, a numerical value is given each factor (say from 1 to 10); the numerical values are added up, averaged, and a single numerical rating is given each person interviewed.

Understandably, the interview process offers many opportunities for discrimination, even with interviewers who try to be unbiased. Consider the criteria suggested by one governmental publication: "temperament, use of English, gestures and bearing . . . appearance, courtesy, and ability to grasp ideas."[21] With the possible exception of ability

[21] George Rosencrans, *Apprenticeship Handbook for Educators* (Sacramento: California State Department of Education, Bureau of Industrial Education, 1962), p. 73

to grasp ideas, all these factors are inevitably judged in terms of cultural norms.

The Final Decision

The final stage in the selection process can be handled almost mechanically (New York regulations require that it be so). Test scores, interview scores, and those based on "objective criteria," such as years of school, can be suitably weighted and added together. If there are ten apprentice vacancies, the ten applicants with the highest scores are accepted into the program, a few others near the top placed on an alternate list, and the rest rejected. Having completed its interviews, the JAC has no further discretion.

The situations observed were not so mechanical, and considerable leeway was allowed for personal judgment. Thus, before its decision meeting, the JAC in one trade was provided by its coordinator with a summary sheet listing each candidate's name, age, education, test scores, interview score, a "total" of the test and interview scores, and "comments," such as "two years at University," "good Navy experience," "shy," "poor eyesight," or "son of member." In this case, apart from the standard preference then given to sons, the decisions were generally consistent with the score totals, as the accompanying table indicates.

What did the JACs look for, both in their interviews and in the final selection?[22] Among the factors considered (in addition to whether the applicant is a son) are the following:

[22] For a discussion of factors considered by JACs, see Brighton, "Apprentice Selection Practices."

	Sons		Not Sons		
Total Score	Accepted	Rejected	Accepted	Alternate List	Rejected
70+			8	1	
60–69	3	0	4	2	1
50–59	2	0		1	12
40–49	3	0			11
Under 40					5

Fixed purpose Does he really want to enter the trade, or is he just trying it out? Will he stick to it, or is he just a job hopper?

Interest in manual work Does he like to work with his hands? Does he like the outdoors? Relevant evidence here includes hobbies, scouting, tinkering with cars, and so forth.

Experience and education Among the favorable indicators are jobs in the construction or building supply fields (in the case of building trades programs), training in the armed services, "good" vocational courses (courses at "bad" schools may detract), and post–high school courses.

Obviously the final weighting of these factors is a matter of personal taste. In one case, for example, a JAC member asked a colleague why he had rated one applicant so low, pointing out that "he is going to school [in our trade] at night. He brought his books here to show us what he was doing. He seemed like a good talker and fairly competent to me." The other member answered, "Here is a man who's 23 years of age. By the time he finishes he will be 27 and have real responsibilities. He's 23 and he's never worked with his hands or at a trade in his life."

A major cause of dispute among committee members concerns the relative weight to be given to intellectual ability. Younger committee members point to what they see as a constantly increasing need for book learning to keep up with the trade—for an understanding of mathematics, theory, and (where relevant) building codes. Older members tend to discount intellectual ability and to feel that experience and a desire to work with one's hands are all-important. "I don't want kids so bright they cause trouble," an employer of cement masons commented. "I want a kid who will do the job I tell him." An employer of molders and coremakers reported similarly: "Our work is so dirty I'd be afraid of taking a good man on because he'd quit."

Centralism and Formalism

Apprenticeship selection has become increasingly centralized and formalized in recent years. Though nepotism, patronage, and bias still enter the picture, there is an increasing tendency for JACs to make selections on the basis of tests and structured interviews. Instead of apprentices' being selected by business agents or individual employers on the basis of casual impressions, the selection process seems to be moving toward what President Schoemann of the Plumbers once sneeringly called the "so-called 'merit' system."[23]

Recent antidiscrimination regulations requiring selection to be made using the criteria of "objective standards susceptible to review" have done much to introduce formal-

[23] Peter Schoemann, "Report from the General President," *United Association Journal* 78 (September 1963): 57.

ism. But the trend toward formalism antedates these regulations considerably. As early as 1961, in northern California, there was a noticeable tendency toward centralized selection and even toward preapprenticeship schooling,[24] both elements of "rational selection" not required by antidiscrimination regulations. Other explanations must be sought.

To get the monkey off the business agent's back One reason for the greater formality is that it makes the business agent's job easier.[25] True, some business agents look upon apprenticeship openings as patronage plums to be handed out to political friends. But this has its disadvantages. "For every friend you make this way," a business agent commented, "you make several enemies." Though the distribution of apprenticeship jobs is a source of political power, it is also a "headache" (as more than one union leader put it). Thus, a well-entrenched business agent was defeated in a membership revolt, and a major reason, according to several reliable observers, was resentment of his distribution of apprenticeship openings. Formalization of selection procedures lessens pressures of this sort; in the words of one business agent, "it takes the monkey off my back." Others made similar comments.

Formal selection proceedings make it possible to turn down incompetent sons (the business agent can always ex-

24 This tendency has been accompanied by stricter enforcement of regulations requiring school attendance and on-the-job rotation.

25 For a discussion of how formalism protects business agents from membership pressures in the operation of hiring halls, see George Strauss, *Unions in the Building Trades* (Buffalo: University of Buffalo, 1957), pp. 157–158.

plain to an irate parent whose son was refused admission to the program that the boy's test grades were so bad that other members of the JAC adamantly refused to admit him). Similarly, formal selection can take pressure off employers. An automotive mechanics business agent explained the poor quality of apprentices in his program before centralized selection by "the fact that the employers take apprentices into the program as a favor to customers or friends; possibly a customer comes in and buys five trucks and then the employer returns this favor by putting his boy to work in the apprenticeship program."

Selection of better candidates Unions and employers have found that formalized selection procedures can lead to marked improvements in apprentice quality, thus benefiting both parties. To take a dramatic (and hardly typical) example, dropout rates during the first nine months of apprenticeship were reduced from 80 to less than 10 percent after the East Bay Auto Mechanics JAC introduced a centralized selection system.

The small employers who predominate in most of the apprenticeable trades lack the facilities or know-how to evaluate job applicants. They can quickly learn whether journeymen are qualified by trying them out on the job. In the case of apprentices, aptitude is what is important, and this is hard to determine immediately. Thus formalized selection can perform a service for the employer by improving the quality of the men he hires.

Formalized selection also helps the union. In unions where selection is lax, there are often large numbers of incompetent apprentices who have been laid off by their original employers and who are hard to place with other employers, thus making the business agent's job much more difficult.

Status A final point is that tight selection standards seem to have become status symbols among the trades. The tighter and more involved the admissions procedure, the higher the status of the trade, or so tradesmen like to believe.

Conclusion

Let us now return to our initial questions. Do apprenticeship selection policies restrict entry excessively? Do they operate to discriminate unfairly against minorities?

Excessive restriction The first question can be disposed of quickly, though not to everyone's satisfaction, not even my own. Union apprentice rules, in my opinion, do not *substantially* restrict supply. I argue as follows:[26]

1. Ratio rules are only slightly restrictive, since the vast majority of employers have fewer apprentices than the rules permit and the rules themselves are frequently lifted in times of labor shortage.

2. Quotas are set on the basis of a conservative estimate of the market's ability to absorb apprentices. In the situation observed, despite this conservative bias, there were often apprentices "on the bench" during most of the year.

3. Any restrictive impact of apprenticeship rules is reduced by the fact that most journeymen enter through the back door. Restrictions on both apprenticeship and back-door

[26] For a roughly equivalent analysis, see Lloyd Reynolds, *Labor Economics and Labor Relations,* 4th ed. (Englewood Cliffs, N.J.: Prentice-Hall, 1964), pp. 188–191.

entry (as in Union H) squeeze supply, but restrictions on apprenticeship alone tend to increase the number who get their training through other means.

4. My limited observations agree with those of Kerr: craft "unions do not generally use their control over the supply of labor to force up wage rates. They employ it rather to adjust supply to demand once the wage has been fixed. . . . Control over supply is used more to preserve the integrity of the wage rate rather [sic] than to create it. The wage rate determines supply more than supply the wage rate."[27] Thus, assuming these observations are accurate, union apprenticeship and admission policies react to rather than create labor market conditions.

5. On balance, union policies may encourage apprenticeship more than they restrict it. Union-enforced JAC pressures raise the quality of training in apprenticeship, and informal union "arm twisting," mentioned earlier, is significant in helping to place apprentices. Centralized selection procedures restrict employer choice, but by providing at least slightly better-qualified candidates, they may lead to the employment of more apprentices. Indeed, I would guess that without union support (or very strong employers' association support), formalized training such as apprenticeship would be hard pressed to survive in any industry characterized by large numbers of small employers. For

[27] Clark Kerr, "The Balkanization of the Labor Market," in E. Wright Bakke et al., *Labor Mobility and Economic Opportunity* (New York: Technology Press and John Wiley & Sons, 1954), pp. 106–107. His observations receive strong support from Gordon W. Bertram, *Consolidated Bargaining in California Construction,* University of California, Institute of Industrial Relations Monograph no. 12 (Berkeley, 1966).

example, apprenticeship as such is practically nonexistent in the nonunion sector of the printing and construction industries.

Admission procedures How fair are apprenticeship selection procedures, particularly the formalistic ones? Do they pick the best possible candidates for apprenticeship? Do they discriminate unfairly, particularly against minority groups?

To start with, how do these selection procedures compare with those used in the manufacturing industry? Certainly the testing procedure is at least as elaborate as that used by most companies in selecting blue-collar workers. To be sure, there has been too little validation of selection procedures, and it would seem that too much emphasis has been given in some trades to intellectual ability rather than to interests or mechanical aptitude. But similar criticisms could be made of many industrial programs.[28]

The interview procedures also differ from those used by most industrial programs. Industrial personnel directors are trained in techniques such as nondirective interviewing. JAC members are untrained. But perhaps the biggest difference is that applicants are interviewed by a large committee instead of by a single person. On the one hand, this

[28] A recent federal regulation, which applies to federal contractors and subcontractors in both construction and manufacturing, requires (with certain exceptions) that all tests be validated in terms of the specific jobs that are being filled and in accordance with standard psychological procedures. *Federal Register,* September 24, 1968, pp. 14392—14394. As an employers' group suggests, "one clear result of vigorous enforcement of the Department of Labor's order will be that many contractors will simply feel compelled to drop testing." Machinery & Allied Products Institute, Memorandum IR–18, October 9, 1968, p. 10.

has the advantage of providing pooled judgment, which may balance the prejudices and idiosyncrasies of the single person. On the other hand, the large committee tends to overawe the applicant who has little experience in job hunting (unless he has friends on the committee who make him feel more at ease).

But is the system fair to blacks? How about the building trades' long tradition of nepotism? "It has been historic over the years," C. J. Haggerty, president of the AFL-CIO Building and Construction Trades Department, told a congressional committee, "that you become an apprentice boy in a given trade . . . by being a brother or son or cousin of a member, or of an employer or management. . . ."[29] It was also traditional that apprenticeship slots not given to relatives were reserved for those with "sponsors." As a result, some construction locals were dominated by a single nationality. Sometimes not being Italian or Irish was almost as much a cause for exclusion as being black.

The new rationalized, centralized forms of selection have reduced (but not completely eliminated) the instances of outright favoritism. Nepotism, it is generally agreed, is much less widespread than it was only five years ago. However, blacks are underrepresented not merely because of favoritism. Even without preference, sons have an advantage. They know how and where to apply for jobs. They have contacts among employers and business agents. They

[29] U.S. Congress, House Committee on Labor and Education, Special Subcommittee on Labor, *Hearings on H.R. 8219,* 87th Cong., 1st sess. (1961), p. 138. Haggerty estimated that at least 50 percent of apprentices fell in this class (perhaps a high estimate at that time).

have learned the nomenclature of the trade, and many have actually worked with its tools. Even those who first look for jobs elsewhere always keep the trade in mind as a possible source of employment. Blacks have none of these advantages. Rarely do they think in terms of entering the trades. They do not know of the existence of apprenticeship vacancies or where to apply to fill them. At least until recently, they have received little help in this regard, either from their school counselors or from the employment service. They have little worthwhile experience to bring the employer. As a consequence, until recently very few applied for admission.[30]

Actually, the rationalization of selection standards, as required by antidiscrimination regulations, may have done more to reduce nepotism and favoritism than to increase minority representation. Even "objective" procedures may be discriminatory. The tightened residency and education requirements plus the disqualification of those with criminal records together screen out more blacks than whites (and in some cases were undoubtedly designed to do so). Tests too may be unfair. Not only may they be culturally biased, but they may test for traits that are not central to apprenticeship success. Many tests measure scholastic aptitude rather than potential as a craftsman (although it can be argued that scholastic aptitude is important, since apprentices must take substantial classroom work). Since white boys may have more experience working with machinery than black ones, they may have an (unfair?) advantage on

30 For numerous case studies, see Ray Marshall and Vernon Briggs, Jr., *The Negro and Apprenticeship* (Baltimore: Johns Hopkins Press, 1967).

mechanical aptitude tests (here, too, such experience may be relevant to success as an apprentice).

New York probably goes furthest to ensure color blindness. In the interests of objectivity they require admission procedures to be made mechanically, on the basis of total scores. Tests are limited to those "developed and administered by competent [outside] organizations."[31] Interviews are restricted to 25 percent of the total weight. Furthermore, there must be "a written formulation of objective criteria by which the interviewer is to judge applicants, and the interviewer shall prepare and maintain a written evaluation of the applicant in terms of the criteria." Finally, in one case, the New York State Human Relations Commission ruled that "evaluation [of the interview] must be made by an independent and professionally competent expert who must be certified as a psychologist under the State Education law."[32] The stringency of these regulations (and their interpretation) may have contributed to the decision of five New York area construction locals to determine admission on the basis of date application and of another four to decide it on the basis of a public drawing, thus giving up all efforts to exercise discretion.

31 Apprentices Training Regulations, 12 NYCRR IX (A), Sec. 600.3 (c), (September 1, 1964). These regulations are less stringent than the recently adopted federal regulations for contractors.

32 Bureau of National Affairs, *Daily Labor Report,* February 8, 1968, p. A–2. This pronouncement, though sounding like a requirement for all apprenticeship programs, was, of course, made in the context of a single case of discrimination. The commission also questioned whether in choosing people for training in a manual craft, heavy weight should be given to factors like experience, military service, and college education.

One wonders whether the New York regulations may be too restrictive in their pursuit of the will-o'-the-wisp of color-blind selection. Marshall and Briggs argue with considerable justification that such measures generally have reached the point of declining returns and that, therefore, fewer efforts should be given to changing admission practices and more to increasing the number and qualifications of black applicants.[33] The experience of the Workers Defense League with the New York Sheet Metal case illustrates that tests need not be an insurmountable barrier. But the WDL program involves more than a cram school to help blacks pass exams. WDL also engages in an active recruiting campaign, it chaperones applicants through various stages of the selection procedure, and it coaches them to do well. By fall 1968 programs similar to this had been funded in 44 industrial areas and have placed over 1650 blacks in apprenticeship.

In some cases neither color blindness nor recruitment may be enough. Though there has been good progress in bringing blacks into apprenticeship, particularly in the last two years, much still needs to be done. The progress to date is largely the result of pressures from the government and civil rights groups. If further progress is to be made, increasing pressure may be required.[34] For federal contractors in most branches of industry today, the test of compliance

[33] *The Negro and Apprenticeship.*

[34] The New York program may possibly be viewed as an example of governmental pressure or even harassment. Thus the apprenticeship program of Local 3, IBEW, which does admit substantial numbers of blacks, is allowed to operate under quite vague standards; by contrast, lily-white programs are held to stringent rules.

with affirmative action programs is no longer absence of discrimination; it is the actual presence of blacks on the payroll. In dealing with apprenticeship, at least with government contractors, the test should also be that of results; the method of selection is secondary so long as it leads to black faces on the job. In the past it was standard practice in many of the building trades to give preference to sons and relatives; it might well be justified today to give equal preference to blacks until the present imbalance is somewhat redressed.

Present admission standards (such as high school graduation) may be too stringent. In many trades excessive emphasis is being placed on "objective" standards, such as the results of unvalidated tests. Of course, the trades argue with considerable justification that the basic criterion for selection should be merit. But since we are not sure that present practices do in fact lead to selecting the best men—and we do know they tend to weed out blacks—perhaps these practices should be suspended, at least for the current "urban crisis emergency."

Thus I find myself in considerable agreement with the latest position of President Schoemann of the Plumbers when he attacks the mechanical point system:[35]

> If affirmative action, which is a very "color conscious" approach, is the right social policy for our times, then why must minority recruits be run through some kind of "color blind" point competition? . . . I . . . advocate waiving existing entrance requirements . . . but solely . . . when joint

[35] Peter T. Schoemann, "Apprenticeship and Fresh Air," *UA Journal* 80 (August 1968): 56–57.

apprenticeship committees [do] not find any applicants of the minority race who fulfilled all the advertised requirements.

In fact, as of fall 1968, some government contracting agencies were applying the criterion of results rather than method of selection. In other words, they were trying to force each contractor to hire minimum quotas of blacks in each trade. Others were satisfied as long as the method of selection was color-blind.

To summarize: union apprenticeship admission policies do not seem to be greatly restrictive in terms of numbers admitted. Substantial progress has been made in reducing favoritism and discrimination in selection procedures. Further progress may require some sort of temporary quota system.[36]

[36] This essay was first prepared in 1968 and does not take into account the extensive developments since that date, such as the Philadelphia Plan.

5

Public Policy and Labor Relations in Postwar Japan

Solomon B. Levine

The growth of labor unions and the spread of collective bargaining in present-day Japan owe much to the efforts of the Allied Occupation (1945–1952) to implant industrial democracy as part of its massive reform of Japanese society. At the time of the surrender, Japan had no labor movement and no collective bargaining. Today, union membership is about 11 million, unions number more than 50,000, and collective agreements cover 7 million unionists. These sizable accomplishments have developed within the context of a public policy initially derived from American experience. The Occupation, almost exclusively American in conception and execution, looked primarily to U.S. institutions for its model for democratic reform and applied the framework of American law to Japanese industrial relations. Positive encouragement of industrial democracy, based on worker self-organization and free union-management bargaining, drew its chief inspiration from New Deal legislation. Just as the measures from the Norris-LaGuardia Act to the Wagner Act had been a response to the need for change in American industry in the 1930s,[1] so the basic principles of these measures appeared suitable for the enormous experiment in economic, social, and political reform of postwar Japan.

The purpose of this essay is to follow the main outlines of Japanese public policy toward labor-management relations

1 See Douglass V. Brown and Charles A. Myers, "Historical Evolution," in *Public Policy and Collective Bargaining,* ed. Joseph Shister, Benjamin Aaron, and Clyde W. Summers (New York: Harper & Row, 1962), pp. 1–27.

as it has evolved since the inception of the reforms twenty-three years ago. In this field, as in other areas of social change, Japan has been a unique testing ground for the "exportability" of public policy from one nation to another. As Myers has pointed out,[2] it is doubtful whether most aspects of an industrial relations system can be transplanted without modification across national boundaries, and so one would expect that in the Japanese case adjustment to foreign conditions led to significant alterations in the original policy. This essay also explores the reasons for such changes. The concluding remarks comment briefly on Japanese public policy formation and the prospects for future policy changes regarding labor relations in that country.

Beginnings

When the Allied powers occupied Japan in September 1945, the outlook for autonomous labor unionism and free collective bargaining in Japanese industry was not promising. The scant history of organized labor in presurrender Japan, although it could be traced back as early as the turn of the century, offered a meager basis for the growth of labor unions on a large scale. While the 1920s had witnessed a brief period of "liberalism" toward worker self-organization and union-management negotiations, the controlling powers hovered somewhere between suppression and toleration in their attitude and policy. Major industrialists responded by

[2] Charles A. Myers, "The American System of Industrial Relations: Is It Exportable?" *Proceedings of the Fifth Annual Meeting,* Industrial Relations Research Association, December 1963, pp. 2–14.

stepping up paternalism in a way that allowed little worker independence in dealing with management. With the ascendancy of the militarists to power after 1931, industrial democracy was removed entirely from serious consideration, and by the end of the thirties the government had driven what few unions there were out of existence and had established a comprehensive, monolithic labor front for direct control of the work force, reflecting the ultranationalistic fervor that supported military adventurism.[3]

Following the collapse of the wartime government, the initiative for generating democratic reform in Japan lay almost entirely with the Occupation authorities. There were few elements in the Japanese caretaker administration after the surrender who were more than vaguely familiar with the ingredients of democracy, such as an autonomous labor movement. Moreover, the economy was in ruins and industrial management in a state of paralysis. However, the initial objectives of the Occupation were clear-cut. First was to stamp out all vestiges of militarism, a task largely achieved within a few months. Second was to democratize Japan so pervasively that "scarcely a major sector of Japanese society was left untouched." This, of course, was far more complex than demilitarization and became the con-

[3] For reviews of Japanese labor unionism and industrial relations in the prewar as well as the postwar period, see Iwao Ayusawa, *A History of Labor in Modern Japan* (Honolulu: East-West Center Press, 1966); Solomon B. Levine, *Industrial Relations in Postwar Japan* (Urbana: University of Illinois Press, 1958); Kazuo Okochi, *Labor in Modern Japan* (Tokyo: Science Council of Japan, Division of Economic, Commerce, and Business Administration, 1958); and Robert A. Scalapino, "Japan," in *Labor and Economic Development,* ed. Walter Galenson (New York: John Wiley & Sons, 1959), pp. 75–145.

stant preoccupation of the Supreme Commander for the Allied Powers (SCAP) until the signing of the Treaty of San Francisco in September 1951.[4]

Under the terms of the unconditional surrender, SCAP possessed plenary powers for initiating reform programs, subject only to the general directives of the President of the United States as commander in chief. The authority of SCAP had no challengers. It faced little competition from governmental agencies within the United States or from the other Allied powers. There was virtually no resistance to its commands from the prostrate Japanese government. Thus, democracy was bestowed "from above" rather than being left to evolve from the experience of the Japanese themselves. This contradiction between the nature of democracy and the means by which it was fostered marked most of the reforms of the Occupation and was especially pronounced in the industrial relations area, where authoritarianism had been so strongly entrenched.

Actually SCAP's overriding control of the implantation of democracy was tempered by a high degree of benevolence and tolerance of trial and error, for throughout the Occupation it relied upon the existing governmental machinery of Japan to carry out its "suggestions." Although the Occupation quickly worked out its basic policies for democratization and began to implement them within a year after the surrender, SCAP's approach was to see how they worked out in practice and to make modifications in light of the

[4] See Robert E. Ward, "Reflections on the Allied Occupation and Planned Political Change in Japan," in *Political Development in Modern Japan,* ed. Robert E. Ward (Princeton, N.J.: Princeton University Press, 1968), pp. 477–535.

results. Labor reform followed the same course of development, so that it was not until the early 1950s that Japanese public policy toward labor-management relations became definitive.

Labor reforms were among the first proclaimed by the Occupation. Within days after the signing of the surrender, the White House issued its first policy directive to SCAP, stating among other things that "encouragement shall be given and favor shown to the development of organizations in labor, industry, and agriculture, organized on a democratic basis." By December 1945, with the direction and approval of SCAP, the Japanese government adopted a far-reaching Trade Union Law (TUL). Not only was the TUL the first of its kind in Japanese history, it was also sweeping in its guarantees of labor rights. All workers—with the exception of police, firemen, prison guards, and other public safety personnel—now had the unqualified right to organize unions of their own choosing, to engage in collective bargaining with employers, and to resort to acts of dispute, including strikes. Drawing almost word for word from the Wagner Act, the TUL prohibited employers under threat of penalty from engaging in unfair labor practices that might interfere with these rights. It also established equally representative tripartite labor relations commissions at national and prefectural levels to assist workers in forming unions and carrying on collective bargaining, process unfair practice charges, and help settle labor-management disputes. At the same time, SCAP set up its own unit to encourage labor organization and ordered the release from jail of all political prisoners, including the prewar labor leaders, who were urged to take the helm in launching the new labor movement. By Occupation order the wartime labor front was immediately dissolved.

In September 1946 a companion piece of legislation, the Labor Relations Adjustment Law (LRAL), went into effect. This act spelled out the procedures for appointing the tripartite labor relations commissions, requiring labor and management to approve not only each other's representatives but the public members also. It also set forth detailed rules for registering unions, processing unfair labor practice cases, and providing conciliation, mediation, and voluntary arbitration in disputes. The main thrust of the measure was to emphasize voluntarism and to minimize if not eliminate government intervention in labor relations. It incorporated only one restriction in requiring a thirty-day cooling-off period before resort to strikes in "public welfare" industries (specified as including rail transportation, postal service, telephone and telegraph, water, gas, electricity, medicine, and public health—most of which at that time were government operated). Adoption of this provision appears to have been influenced by the then-current labor problems in the United States as well by the dire straits of the Japanese economy itself. Also added to the few groups denied the basic rights of labor under the TUL were civil servants in government judicial and administrative agencies, but almost immediately the Japanese Cabinet declared that employes of the government-owned railroads, post offices, telecommunications and certain other public enterprises, as well as public school teachers and lower-ranked members of the civil service, were exempt from these categories.

The two pieces of legislation taken together represented almost a complete absence of constraint upon labor. While the policy was reminiscent of the high point of governmental liberalism toward trade unions in the United States represented by the Thornhill case in 1940, it actually went further, since government officials and employers, uncertain of their status and in constant risk of prosecution and purge as war criminals, offered virtually no resistance. To gain favor with the Occupation, most were ready to assist workers in establishing unions, gaining recognition for them, and concluding collective bargaining agreements. Unlike the New Deal period, in which many American employers fought the policy of positive encouragement to unionism and collective bargaining, in the period immediately after the war Japanese management essentially abandoned any claims to its prerogatives.

The Labor Standards Law (LSL) enacted in April 1947 completed the foundations of the new Japanese labor policy. This act incorporated a wide spectrum of minimum protections for workers designed to assure the end of labor exploitation by employers, public and private, and brought Japanese industry abreast of most of the resolutions regarding working conditions adopted by the ILO. By the following August, reorganization of the governmental administrative apparatus had established a Ministry of Labor for the first time in Japan to take responsibility for enforcing the labor reforms and provide a voice for labor within a government now based, under the new Constitution, on the sovereignty of the people rather than a deitylike emperor.

The Constitution, framed in November 1946 and promulgated in April 1947, underwrote the labor policy embodied in the TUL, LRAL, and LSL. Its omnibus "bill of rights" included, among other provisions, "freedom of assembly and association as well as speech, press, and other forms of expression" (Article 21), a guarantee "to maintain minimum standards of wholesome and cultural living" for all citizens (Article 25), and "the right of workers to organize and to bargain and to act collectively" (Article 28).

All these measures were designed to make organized labor into a major countervailing force within Japanese society in order to prevent the resurgence of oligarchical control and authoritarianism on the part of government and employers. The labor response, in fact, exceeded most expectations. Instead of beginning slowly to develop unionism and collective bargaining relations, workers rushed to heed the call of the Occupation. As I mentioned earlier, many elements of government and management encouraged them to do so and in some cases themselves joined in the new labor organizations, creating an atmosphere not unlike the unity of the wartime labor front. Measured in numbers of unionists and unions, "General MacArthur wants you to join" probably proved a more effective appeal than the CIO leadership's invocation in the 1930s of President Roosevelt's similar wish. Within a few months after Japan's surrender, at least 5 million workers were members of the more than 17,000 unions that had registered with the labor relations commissions. Collective bargaining, too, suddenly seemed vigorous, especially in light of the fact that before the war it had hardly been practiced and had seldom been concluded with written agreements. By 1947, signed labor-management contracts covered more than 5000 unions and a year later 20,000, with close to 80 percent of the 6.7 million organized workers. Most agreements readily conceded union recognition, provided union security clauses, and granted dues checkoffs. In 1946, almost 1000 labor disputes broke out, the bulk of them involving strikes, with more than 2.7 million participants—a sharp contrast to the prewar peak of 350,000 participants in any single year.

These indicators appeared to justify the Occupation's objective of developing labor unions as a countervailing force. Moreover, they seemed to demonstrate that Japanese labor eagerly sought industrial democracy once it was released from the shackles of an authoritarianism that had justified worker submissiveness as part of the social harmony and familialism of traditional Japan.

Reform and Reaction

The initial public policy toward labor in the new Japan should not be understood as a carbon copy of U.S. policy. Only the basic injunctions were imported. Encouragement of labor organization, guaranteed rights to organize, bargain, and strike, and protection against unfair employer practices were part of the effort to refashion the whole political, social, and economic structure of Japan and to introduce a new ethos into Japanese society. The complexities of American labor relations law and its administration, which then centered on "balancing" worker and management rights and were about to lead to the passage of the Taft-Hartley Act, could be easily ignored.

There were at least two major departures from the American approach. One, essentially "overshooting" U.S. policy, was the blanket guarantee of the new labor rights to virtually all workers, except for the few noted, without distinguishing between the public and private sectors of employment. This was not an oversight by any means, but part of a conscious attempt to develop a labor movement to counter governmental authority, as well as that of private employers. While SCAP rejected socialism for Japan, it did accept an assertive role for workers in the operation of public agencies and private enterprises, for the government and private industry had been closely intertwined during the rise of Japanese totalitarianism. Moreover, since the government was an important employer itself through its ownership and direct operation of certain major services and industrial monopolies, the Occupation wished to make it a "model" for the private sector regarding relations with employees. Public workers, who eventually came to comprise at least one-fourth of organized labor and to form some of the largest and best-organized unions, responded immediately to the new freedoms. This response was not to be discouraged.

Another major departure was a heavier emphasis on worker participation in the direct framing and execution of policy. The Occupation opened the way to the formation of labor-based political parties, most of radical ideological bent, and urged a system of proportional representation in the Diet to assure a legislative role for these groups. In the labor relations laws themselves, special stress was placed upon tripartitism in the composition and functioning of the labor relations commissions. The notion of a public-member-only NLRB was rejected, since it did not provide direct labor participation in the administration of the new laws. Far more relevant was the experience with tripartitism in the ILO or on the U.S. War Labor Board. Tripartitism was also compatible with Japanese legislation of the late 1920s which provided for conciliation and mediation in labor disputes.

Since the principal aims were to promote formation of independent unions in whatever form, questions about appropriate bargaining units, exclusive representation rights, and conducting union representation elections were of little concern at this point. Nor was there worry about the consequences of rivalry among union organizations with different organizational philosophies. The TUL and LRAL were intended to produce a revolution in the industrial decision-making process rather than to force employers simply to accept the legitimacy of labor unionism within an established managerial system. In this sense, the Japanese reforms probably represented a sharper upheaval than the New Deal.

Indeed, the labor reforms were so revolutionary that they soon mounted a serious challenge to the very authority of SCAP itself when, early in 1947, the major unions called for a general strike. While the decision to stage a general strike arose from a seemingly unending series of widespread wage disputes—fed by rapid inflation, economic disorganization, and governmental budgetary difficulties—fundamentally it reflected two major problems confronting the Occupation. One lay in the need to reconcile with each other the large number of rights that had been suddenly bestowed on the Japanese; the other was an emerging conflict about the basic objectives of the Occupation now that the Cold War had virtually begun. Only the Occupation, with its ultimate powers, could resolve these questions.

The general strike call for February 1, 1947, became the acid test of the limits to which the Occupation would actually allow the labor movement to go in building the New Japan. Could labor's unified strength be allowed to bring down the conservative government in power through direct strike action? Did a general strike unduly trample on the rights of private property and neutral citizens? Did it exceed the acceptable bounds of freedom of expression? These and similar questions[5] were at stake, and with the new Constitution not yet promulgated and little litigation experience accumulated in the courts and administrative agencies, answering them fell to the Occupation authorities.

At the same time, the general strike call came when the United States was reappraising its policy toward Japan in light of the East-West conflict. It was now becoming clear that the rehabilitation of the Japanese economy, perhaps even the remilitarization of Japan, was highly desirable in order to provide a strong industrial base in Asia allied to the Western powers. Not only did a general strike threaten to paralyze an already chaotic economy, but there also loomed the possibility of leftist labor domination of industry. In addition to the widespread economic issues dividing employers and employees, centering mainly on the

[5] For an analysis of the difficulties in applying the new laws, see Kichiemon Ishikawa, "The Regulation of the Employer-Employee Relationship: Japanese Labor Relations Law," in *Law in Japan,* ed. Arthur T. Von Mehren (Cambridge: Harvard University Press, 1963), pp. 439–473.

public workers, the conflict was fed by an intense rivalry between communists and socialists to gain control of the labor movement, which had temporarily united to form a joint struggle committee to conduct the general strike. Were the general strike to succeed, the economic and political stability SCAP now sought for Japan's industrial resuscitation might be threatened.

SCAP's intervention nine hours before the general strike call went into effect signaled the start of a reassessment of policies toward labor-management relations in Japan that continued for the next five years. Although the joint committee acceded to SCAP's order to cancel the call and dissolve itself, the episode left a number of issues unresolved, and they have remained so up to the present. They focused on restrictions on labor rights, especially for the public sector employees, and the degree of participation actually permitted labor in industrial decision making—the two cardinal points of Occupation policy designed to lead to the democratization of industrial relations.

Reassessment of Labor Policies

In effect, SCAP's prohibition of the general strike severely curtailed, if it did not prohibit, stoppages by government worker unions. It also threw the validity of collective agreements in the public sector into doubt. Clarification of the public employee's status began in the summer of 1948 only after government unions had once again resorted to a rash of localized stoppages which the national unions threatened to "coordinate." Following a stern warning to the national unions came General MacArthur's letter to the Japanese government in July 1948 "suggesting" that new laws be enacted to deal with the bargaining and strike rights of public employees. These suggestions were immediately incorporated in Cabinet Order 201, by the end of the year in revisions of the National Public Service Law (NPSL) adopted a year earlier, and in a new Public Corporation Labor Relations Law.

Essentially, these acts removed government workers from coverage by the TUL and LRAL. However, a major distinction was made between civil servants and workers in government-owned enterprises. For the former, the NPSL, which originally had no restrictions on labor rights beyond those contained in the LRAL, was revised to limit units of civil service workers—defined by the National Personnel Authority (NPA)—to the right to organize. While civil servants' organizations could be granted the privilege of "negotiating" with government agencies, they were prohibited from concluding collective agreements and resorting to work stoppages. The NPA now had exclusive responsibility for drawing up recommendations for the terms and conditions of work for civil servants and for submitting them to the Cabinet and Diet for approval.

The new law for the public enterprises, later retitled the Public Corporation and National Enterprise Labor Relations Law (PCNELRL) after the reorganization of several government operations, permitted these workers the right to organize and conclude collective agreements but denied them the right to strike. Moreover, their units had to be made up only of workers in these operations, and a union had to select its officers from its membership. Negotiations were limited to wages and working conditions and could not deal with managerial operations. To settle disputes, special tripartite machinery was established to provide conciliation, mediation, and arbitration, and under most circumstances public member mediation or arbitration was made compulsory. Included in this category were the national railways, printing office, mint, and alcohol and tobacco monopolies; the postal and telecommunications services and some other agencies were added in 1951.

On the one hand, the treatment of the Japanese public workers did not go as far as the Taft-Hartley Act had in the case of federal employees in the United States only a year earlier. Government workers retained some of the rights the Occupation had initially granted, and it is worth noting that an attempt was made to distinguish among different groups of public employees with regard to their legitimate labor activities. On the other hand, whereas government unions were not a highly significant element of American organized labor, in Japan they were one of its major segments. As a result, the restrictions, which sought to separate government workers from the unions in the private sector, dealt a serious blow to the infant Japanese labor movement's attempt to achieve political and economic solidarity.

Once the status of the public workers was redefined, the government turned to a major revision of the original Trade Union Law and the Labor Relations Adjustment Law, which now applied mainly to the private sector. The amendments, adopted in June 1949, attempted to curtail politically oriented union activity and to reduce the influence of national labor organizations on the rank and file. Following the example of the Taft-Hartley Act, the changes stiffened the tests for union autonomy and democracy in internal union affairs. Instead of the mere registration that had been provided for under the original TUL, all unions were now required to submit themselves to qualifications examinations by the public members of the labor relations commissions in order to receive the protections and benefits of the law. Although, unlike the Taft-Hartley Act, the amendments did not specify a set of union unfair labor practices, the qualifications examination approached the idea of protecting individual workers, especially at the lowest organizational level, against their officers and against domination by upper-level union bodies.

Probably the most important effect of the changes was to weight the administration of labor rights in favor of union organizations at the enterprise rather than at the industrial or national levels. Since this increased the risk of the unions' falling under management control, especially in view of Japan's long history of close employer-employee identification within a given firm, the protections against employer interference were also strengthened, partly through the new qualifications examination and partly through more precise prohibitions against employer unfair labor practices, such as financial support of unions. In addition, as a means of speeding up cases, only the public members of the labor relations commissions were to decide unfair labor practice charges brought to them.

Thus, the thrust of the amendments was to restructure the framework within which organized labor in the private sector pursued its rights to organize, bargain, and engage in disputes. Technically, none of these rights was curtailed, although a change in the LRAL permitted the prime minister, with Diet approval, to add, for up to a year at a time, to the list of "public welfare" industries subject to the thirty-day cooling-off period before they could resort to a strike.

Further administrative and legislative steps were taken from 1949 to 1953 to complete the revised framework for union-management relations. With the outbreak of the Korean War, government and industry "purged" several thousand communists and communist sympathizers from leadership posts at the instruction of the Occupation. This had the effect of further reducing the political involvement of the labor movement and weakening national union organizations. Then, as the signing of the peace treaty for Japan approached, the labor relations laws were subjected to further reexamination to bring them into line with Japanese "realities." The end of the Occupation in April 1952 ushered in still new enactments. A "national emergency" strike procedure, similar in many respects to Taft-Hartley, was adopted, while the thirty-day cooling-off period for public welfare industries was dropped (with a ten-day notification requirement in its stead). As mentioned, various government units, such as the postal services and telegraph and telephone, were transferred from the NPSL to the PCNELRL, but new laws paralleling these were passed applying to local government workers, who presumably had remained under the jurisdiction of Cabinet Order 201 of 1948. Moreover, after prolonged stoppages in coal mining and electric power, the government in 1953 enacted specific legislation curtailing strikes in these industries.

In a sense, the new laws had spun an intricate web of regulations that took the place of SCAP's general strike prohibition. They had differentiated among the various categories of organized labor and had attempted to confine but not to deny the exercise of labor rights. Public policy still encouraged unionism and collective bargaining, but on a highly decentralized and compartmentalized basis. At the same time, given the objectives of rehabilitating the Japanese economy, now about to move into high gear, the policy served to restore management prestige and authority.

Shift to a High-Growth Economy

Until 1965, when the Japanese government under great international and domestic pressure ratified ILO Convention 87 on freedom of association, decentralization in union-management relations remained the principal theme of public labor policy in Japan. It also provided the main bone of contention between the government and the major part of organized labor, which has constantly sought restoraation of the unrestricted rights bestowed in 1945. However, until the ILO 87 ratification, only minor changes were made in the basic legal framework. It was during this period, of course, that Japanese governmental policies were primarily directed toward achieving high rates of economic growth and rapid industrialization. Also, despite episodes such as the mass protest in 1960 over the security agreement with the United States, Japan maintained an extraordinary degree of political stability, with the conservatives remaining in firm control of the government and its policies. Under these conditions, the Japanese pattern of industrial relations tended to congeal. While labor unionism grew steadily, the proportion of workers organized in the industrial labor force dropped from 50 to 35 percent. Enterprise-level unions remained the pervasive organizational type, but unionism was far more successful in the large, modern firms than in the small and medium enterprises.

Although organized labor in Japan strongly protested the restructuring of public policy toward labor relations that occurred from 1947 to 1953, in actuality union reaction was mixed. The changes from the initial policy of unrestrained freedom gave encouragement to "democratization" movements within labor organizations that aided the purge of communists and led to the demise of the communist-dominated national labor center, *Sanbetsu,* in 1950. It also shook up the socialist center, *Sōdōmei,* which thereafter was unable to rid itself of accusations of "boss control" and attract the dissidents from *Sanbetsu* or the "neutral" unions. In effect, what had happened was the ascendancy of labor leadership at the enterprise level. By 1950, it had become clear that the predominant forms of labor unionism in Japan were the enterprise-based organizations, particularly in the large firms and government agencies. From the point of view of a unified labor movement, the danger was that these unions, despite the changes in the law designed to strengthen union autonomy and decrease employer influence, would become too inward-looking. Since enterprise-level unions tended to embrace all the regular workers in the firm, blue- and white-collar alike, and in many cases extended their memberships into the ranks of managerial personnel, their internal administration was apt to be highly complex, mainly concerned with balancing the interests of the different work groups within the enterprise itself, and little aroused by the concerns and problems of labor outside the enterprise proper. At least 80 percent of all unionists were organized on an enterprise basis.[6]

The formation of a new national labor center, *Sōhyō,* in 1950 reflected these basic characteristics. *Sōhyō* attempted to pick up the pieces of the fragmented, compartmentalized labor movement, which by that time was actually losing membership. Its initial appeals, following the revised labor policy (and thus receiving Occupation blessing), stressed internal union democracy, economic action on an industrial basis, avoidance of political involvement, opposition to communism, and intention to affiliate with the newly formed ICFTU. However, *Sōhyō's* efforts to achieve labor unity fell short of success. It was able to gather together only about half of organized labor. Numerous enterprise unions and many of the "neutral" labor organizations and *Sōdōmei* affiliates remained outside, preferring to wait and see how *Sōhyō* would actually develop. Even enterprise unions that chose to join (most through industrial federations) remained skeptical about the usefulness of affiliation, in part because of a public policy that favored decentralization in industrial relations.

It soon became clear to the *Sōhyō* leadership that the effectiveness of the new center depended upon reasserting labor's political interests, defined as securing Japan's neutrality in the Cold War and supporting pacifism, opposing American

[6] Solomon B. Levine, "Japan," in *White-Collar Trade Unionism,* ed. Adolf Sturmthal (Urbana: University of Illinois Press, 1966), pp. 205–260.

military bases in Japan, regaining labor rights to the fullest, and challenging the power of the conservative government and large-scale private industry to determine economic policy. Within a year after its founding, *Sōhyō's* ideological complexion began to change completely. By the end of the Occupation in 1952, its role had become primarily political, it had opened itself to communist infiltration, and it had allied itself closely with the Marxist left-wing socialists. Although this about-face brought on splits and defections within *Sōhyō* which by 1954 had led to the formation of a rival Right-socialist federation, *Zenrō* (today known as *Dōmei*), the conclusion of the leadership of *Sōhyō* was that labor had no choice but to enter the political arena, since economic action at the enterprise level was likely to result in a set of feeble, disparate efforts.

Ideological considerations aside, a major problem facing the national union leadership was to devise a strategy that would combine political and economic action without running the risk of further restrictive legislation. Already the government was threatening to adopt antisubversive activity laws that would strengthen police surveillance in a manner reminiscent of the 1920s and 1930s and whose greatest impact would be on radical unions. Until the late 1950s, the national union organizations were engaged in internal struggles over this strategy, but the election in 1955 of Kaoru Ohta and Akira Iwai to the top *Sōhyō* offices led to the emergence of the present-day approach. Rather than mount the widespread demonstrations and confrontations that their predecessors had attempted (short of general strikes) or fall back upon enterprise-level bargaining and cooperation, which seemed to be *Zenrō* policy, Ohta and Iwai formulated a strategy that would combine the limited interests of the enterprise unions with widespread political protest. In a sense, the approach was to make the most out of what public policy had helped to structure. Its principal form was the "seasonal struggle," an effort essentially to coordinate and direct the common demands of unions both in the private and in the government sectors of the economy without going to the extreme of a general strike, creating a national emergency, or directly flouting the prohibitions on strikes by government workers. While it is led by *Sōhyō,* the struggle has acquired the support of the confederation of neutral unions and, although it is opposed by *Dōmei,* of some of its affiliates as well.

Sōhyō's Spring Wage Offensive became the most significant seasonal struggle,[7] although there were others such as the one at midyear and at year's end over bonus payments. The Spring Offensive is of key importance because April 1, which begins the fiscal year in Japan and coincides with school graduations, is the date for hiring the bulk of the new labor force. It is also the time for granting general wage increases within enterprises, setting the hiring-in wage, and raising the wages of regular individual workers on the basis of length of service—all issues of vital interest within the enterprise unions themselves. The labor movement has

[7] Robert Evans, Jr., "Shuntō: Japanese Labor's Spring Wage Offensive," *Monthly Labor Review* 90 (October 1967): 23–28. For an analysis of the role of the national unions in coordinating the struggles, see Alice H. Cook, *An Introduction to Japanese Trade Unionism* (Ithaca: New York State School of Industrial and Labor Relations, 1966), especially pp. 63–91.

made little effort to alter these institutions but rather has tried to utilize them for gains in wages and benefits at the moment when annual budgets must be finally determined. These decisions, moreover, significantly affect other wage items, such as the amount of the semiannual bonus (which may come to two or three months' wages) and retirement allowances. By catering to these issues and in effect perpetuating the predominant interests of enterprise unionism, *Sōhyō* and its adherents maximize the strength of the labor organizations both in collective bargaining and in political campaigns.

The usual pattern of the offensive is to designate certain key enterprises in major industries, including the government workers, to engage in a series of one- or two-day strikes, announced well in advance. As the season progresses, other groups join the stoppages, so that a succession of strike waves occurs until final settlements are reached. The Spring Offensive will usually begin in March, reach a climax in April, and taper off in May. In the process, the offensive probes for settlements that will set the pattern for organized labor as a whole and even spill over into the unorganized sectors. Throughout the offensive *Sōhyō* publicizes its political slogans and demands, organizes demonstrations before the Diet, and, should there be an election in the offing, utilizes the walkouts for political rallies.

Although initially *Sōhyō* attempted to achieve the general Spring Offensive wage pattern through public worker union negotiations, the government in most instances has succeeded in avoiding this role in its determination to resist interference with its policies and programs for rapid economic growth. Usually the bargaining has gone into compulsory mediation, with its inevitable delays. The government frequently has refused to accept or has delayed implementation of the terms of mediation awards (or the recommendations of the National Personnel Authority in the case of the civil servants) on budgetary grounds. The result has been a prolongation of public sector disputes through union actions, such as work-to-rule tactics, that are at the very limits of the law, if not outright violations.

The Spring Offensive and other seasonal struggles are thus the product of decentralized and compartmentalized labor relations. They offset what are otherwise relatively untroubled relations between unions and management at the enterprise level. For historical, cultural, and economic reasons analyzed elsewhere,[8] "enterprise," rather than class, occupational, or industrial consciousness characterizes the great majority of the rank-and-file labor organizations, even though they may affiliate with upper bodies at the national level. As a result, many of the most basic decisions still rest with enterprise management, especially recruitment, work force deployment, promotion, wage progression, and a wide range of welfare provisions. In addition to long-standing personnel practices developed by management, there is also the rather comprehensive set of requirements for each firm under the Labor Standards Law, which, although subject to acceptance by the enterprise workers, are policed and approved by the government. Moreover, joint employer-employee councils are frequently utilized for informational

[8] Levine, *Industrial Relations in Postwar Japan,* pp. 101–107.

purposes and adjustment of day-to-day problems, although they are outside the formal bargaining machinery.

The result is a lack of detailed collective bargaining and little use of individual grievance procedures. Collective contracts contain few substantive positions and are often documents that merely reiterate union rights already provided for in the law.[9] As was said earlier, the negotiations themselves tend to focus on the most general issues: across-the-board wage increases, bonuses, and retirement benefits. Even though technological change and increasing labor mobility have begun to break down enterprise compartmentalization in the past few years, the bargaining system is still oriented primarily toward accepting the particularistic character of the individual firm, in which employer and employee are tightly bound together.

Paradoxically, despite untroubled relations and limited bargaining, union-management dealings typically begin with outright confrontation rather than reasoned negotiations and discussion. This is in part the result of the short history of collective bargaining in Japan, but probably it also derives from the need of the enterprise union to demonstrate its solidarity to the employer in as dramatic a fashion as possible. Confrontation tactics thus express the limitations of the union's role in a context where a vast portion of the decisions affecting the work force lies outside the bargaining process itself. Strikes and demonstrations are

[9] Masaichiro Ishizaki, "The Role of the State in Industrial Relations and Modernization: The Changing Nature of Governmental Intervention," in *The Changing Patterns of Industrial Relations* (Tokyo: Japan Institute of Labour, 1965), p. 234.

signals for negotiations to begin rather than the result of breakdowns in negotiations. Labor dispute activity displays a jagged pattern of widespread strikes of short duration at certain periods of the year, with relative quiet and few stoppages at other times. The national labor organizations, recognizing this behavior pattern, utilize confrontation for the seasonal struggles. Without such a strategy, the labor movement would be able to show little unity, bargaining settlements would be highly disparate, and unions would run the risk of even greater employer dominance of industrial relations than already exists.[10]

Nonetheless, unions and management in Japan exhibit a high degree of receptivity to conciliation by third parties, especially the labor relations commissions. Basically, this reflects the aversion of an enterprise's union and its management to prolong their confrontation and to air their disputes in public. It also demonstrates the expectation of a continuous relationship between the employer and his regular workers, perhaps for life. Although the laws provide for formal mediation and arbitration, because of the risks of losing face and even of losing control of enterprise affairs, these laws are seldom utilized except, as noted, in the case of the public sector unions under the PCNELRL.[11]

Within the context of decentralization, the courts have

10 For the internal union problems this poses, see Bernard Karsh and Solomon B. Levine, "Present Dilemmas of the Japanese Labor Movement," *Proceedings of the Spring Meeting,* Industrial Relations Research Association, May 1962, pp. 541–548.

11 Kichiemon Ishikawa, "The Role of Government in Labor Relations in Japan," in *Labor Relations in the Asian Countries* (Tokyo: Japan International Labour Office, 1965).

shown a notably liberal attitude in their interpretation of the labor relations laws. Strikes are not considered interruptions, and workers are entitled to return to their enterprises once settlements are made with their status and benefits fully restored. Picketing, even on a mass basis, is widely tolerated unless violence occurs, for it is accepted as an element in the ongoing employment relationship, rather than being seen purely as a matter of free speech. Similarly, tactics such as the partial strike, scheduled strike, piston strike, and sit-down have not been declared inappropriate. Until 1950, even "production control," in which the workers themselves ran the factories, was not declared an infringement on private property. Employer lockouts are rarely upheld by the courts and run the risk of suits for unpaid back wages because of the doctrine that the employment relationship remains unbroken. The courts, moreover, are the chief recipients of unfair labor practice charges (the law permits resort either to the courts or the labor relations commissions), partly because of the sympathy judges have shown toward labor and partly because it is faster to dispose of cases through court injunctions than through the comparatively slow procedures of the labor relations commissions.[12]

The apparent toleration shown by the courts toward the use of confrontation in union-management bargaining is basically a recognition of the limited and compartmentalized nature of enterprise-level labor relations. Were bargaining carried out on a far wider basis than it is, and were

[12] *Ibid.,* "The Regulation of the Employer-Employee Relationship," pp. 447–460, 464–468.

concerted labor action on an interenterprise scale to occur more frequently, the laws might well come to be interpreted more restrictively. However, this is not likely to be the case as long as present public policy continues to support the decentralized labor relations system.

Labor Relations in Public Employment

Public employment in Japan has provided the setting for a bitter, continuing struggle against a basic public policy favoring decentralization of union-management bargaining. Although the labor unions strenuously objected to enactment of bargaining and strike prohibitions in the NPSL and PCNELRL (and later the amendments to the TUL and the local public employee laws), initially there was little objection to the provisions that confined the jurisdictions of public worker union organizations to given agencies and enterprises and required election of union officers only from the designated membership group. In other words, the new laws applying to government worker unions in effect adopted the American principle of "appropriate" representation units and also ruled out "outside" union leadership. These stipulations appeared acceptable to labor groups at the time because democratization movements within the unions were determined to wrest control from communists and "old-line" labor bosses.

By 1958, however, the public worker unions and the labor centers had begun to challenge this policy as a denial of the right of association and collective bargaining under the Constitution and to claim it was in conflict with ILO Convention 87, which had not however been ratified by the

Japanese government.[13] The first of the events leading up to this challenge occurred when public worker unions, such as the postal workers, national railway workers, local government employees, and teachers, joined *Sōhyō's* seasonal struggle strategy and began to engage in stoppages, work-to-rule movements, and other obstructive activities declared illegal by the government authorities. The government agencies responded by discharging union leaders from their posts and, when the unions refused to replace them with "inside" members, withdrew recognition and declared the agreements null and void. For the labor movement to accept these decisions might have led not only to the weakening of the public worker unions but also to the demise of the entire bargaining and political strategy of *Sōhyō*. Although a temporary compromise was reached through the efforts of the labor relations commission for the public corporations and national enterprises, the public worker unions seized upon the government's actions to focus worldwide attention on the restrictions in the Japanese laws. Complaints filed in Geneva soon led to numerous resolutions by the ILO calling upon Japan to ratify Convention 87 and make appropriate amendments to the relevant labor laws in Japan.

However, despite repeated assertions by the Japanese government that it intended to ratify the Convention, seven years were needed before it was done. Only after the ILO dispatched a three-man panel (the Dryer Committee) of its

[13] For analyses of these events, see Alice H. Cook, "The International Labor Organization and Japanese Politics," *Industrial and Labor Relations Review* 19 (October 1965): 41–57; and Morrison and Marjorie Handsaker, "The ILO and Japanese Public Employees Unions," *Industrial Relations* 7 (October 1967): 80–91.

Fact-Finding and Conciliation Commission on Freedom of Association for an on-the-spot investigation in early 1965 was there a relaxation, if not resolution, of the issue.[14] Following issuance of the panel's report, ratification of the Convention suddenly came in April 1965, accompanied by a set of amendments to the relevant laws that deprived the unions of a number of privileges they had enjoyed. Principal among these were the requirement that continuing full-time union officers give up their government posts within a specified time limit and a redefinition of public employees that eliminated additional "supervisory" categories from eligibility for union membership. The teachers union, for example, was eventually required to exclude the one-tenth of its membership made up of school principals and assistant principals, many of whom had been of critical importance in conducting negotiations on behalf of the union. In addition, while recognizing the right of the public sector unions to have "outside" leadership and affiliation, the government would not concede the right to strike to public employees in any category, or the right to conclude collective agreements to the civil servants.

While this may have been a hollow victory for the unions, the outcome of the ILO Convention 87 issue could eventually have far-reaching public policy implications for Japanese unionism and collective bargaining. The most significant point is that explicit recognition of outside leader-

[14] The full account is available in *Report of the Fact-Finding and Conciliation Commission on Freedom of Association Concerning Persons Employed in the Public Sector in Japan,* mimeograph (Geneva: International Labour Office, 1965).

ship in public policy challenges the predominance of enterprise-centered labor organization and collective bargaining. With ratification of ILO Convention 87, the thrust of the law may strengthen union pressure for supra-enterprise bargaining agreements. Recent trends in the labor market under conditions of rapid economic growth, technological change, and industrialization also increase this likelihood. Mobility has notably increased since around 1960, and wage differentials have been narrowing. If these trends continue, it is not likely that the present highly decentralized system of bargaining would continue to exist indefinitely but rather that there would be a steady shift to formal coordinated bargaining under the aegis of national union leadership.

However, such an outcome would meet obstacles under existing public policy and would have to deal with management resistance and vested interests in enterprise unionism. Questions of the appropriate scope of union membership in all likelihood would become prominent, as they did in revising the public worker labor laws upon ratification of ILO Convention 87. Management would insist upon more specific protection for its "prerogatives," while knotty problems of rank-and-file control over union leadership would have to be resolved as the locus of bargaining moved away from the enterprise.[15] The evolution of collective bargaining in postwar Japan does not hold out great promise for a

[15] These questions are being taken up in exhaustive detail by a special government commission now in the process of reexamining Japanese labor-relations laws and their administration. See *Shūkan Rōdō Niusu* (Weekly Labor News), January 1, 1967, pp. 9–10.

quick resolution of these issues. Instead, one is likely to see a prolonged debate over revising public policy and an increasing resort to "legalism" in union-management relations, which in the view of many is already excessive.

Summary

Although it was transplanted from the United States, public labor relations policy in Japan only partially resembles its progenitor. It has developed into a hybrid showing both Western and Japanese characteristics. As has been commonly observed, this should hardly come as a surprise, since the transplantation occurred before it was known what the economy and political system would eventually look like. There had been little experience with such law and little understanding of its interpretation. The initial objective, inspired mainly by the Occupation, was to achieve thoroughgoing industrial democracy by preventing resurgence of the forces that controlled totalitarian Japan, but this goal soon came into conflict with numerous other civil rights bestowed upon the Japanese, as well as with the drive for rapid economic rehabilitation and growth.

From 1947 until ratification of ILO Convention 87 in 1965, there was a continual chopping away at the basic labor rights initially ordained by the Allied Occupation. The effect of public policy was to contain organized labor and confine union-management collective bargaining. The unions sought a way to regain the offensive within the restrictive arrangements that favored decentralization and enterprise orientation.

The political process for policy formation in Japan is not

conducive to the rapid achievement of changes in law and legal administration that would favor a greater degree of labor unity and coordinated bargaining. A real two-party system has yet to develop. The labor movement has been allied with a minority opposition that is strong enough to prevent major amendments to the Constitution but too weak to take important legislative initiatives.[16] Success in obtaining ratification of ILO Convention 87 came only after seven years of debate and then at the sacrifice of important props for the unions themselves. The conservative government conceded the rights of association but without going so far as to restore all bargaining and strike rights to the public workers, as organized labor demanded. No doubt the government's major motivation in granting this principle was the embarrassment Japan was suffering on the world scene at the very time it was striving to achieve success in international markets. But the concessions were made so as to upset as little as possible the decentralized bargaining system that had emerged in postwar Japan.

"Backsliding" in labor relations policy initially occurred because the unions mounted a challenge to the authority of SCAP itself. When Japan became independent, the conservative government took over the aims of the Occupation, including the overriding objective of rapid economic growth. Yet despite the backsliding, public policy did not revert to the oppression of presurrender Japan. Indeed, it preserved the ideal of industrial democracy, and this ideal,

[16] Robert A. Scalapino and Junnosuke Masumi, *Parties and Politics in Contemporary Japan* (Berkeley: University of California Press, 1962), especially pp. 54–81.

retained in the Constitution and the laws, provides the platform for labor's incessant demand for restoration of its full rights and privileges. By no means should it be concluded that the democratic reforms of Japan's political, economic, and social institutions have been totally lost.

The industrial relations system that emerged in postwar Japan has not been incompatible with the objective of economic growth. Decentralized bargaining arrangements, coupled with the coordinative seasonal struggles, have probably not greatly affected Japan's growth rate. Public policy is designed to keep it that way.

A basic unanswered question, however, is whether full pursuit of the initial Occupation policy toward labor would have made any difference to Japan's economic progress. While no one can tell what might have been, there is little evidence that Japanese unionism could have become so monolithic and centralized as to become a serious impediment to growth. Tradition remained strong, and the notion of enterprise consciousness was not easily changed even with the introduction of Western labor policies. However, it was for these very reasons that the government adopted policies that reinforced traditional characteristics, rather than encouraging the dramatic changes that the Occupation originally envisioned. It remains to be seen whether Japan, as it continues to succeed economically, will turn to promoting self-determination in industrial relations as readily as it has concentrated on economic growth. There are signs that with Japan's increasing affluence, such a development in public policy is a possibility, but one that is likely to evolve slowly under existing economic and political arrangements.

6

Power, Politics, and the Prospects for Collective Bargaining: An Employer Viewpoint

J. W. Miller, Jr.

There is increasingly widespread concern that the collective bargaining process in the United States is sick, so much so that strong therapy may be required. That concern is not without foundation. Some even appear to take the eventual demise of bargaining for granted by prescribing one or more substitutes, such as compulsory arbitration. It is the thesis of this essay that (1) collective bargaining is indeed seriously ill, that (2) the illness need not be fatal, but that (3) it is likely to be so unless effective and timely therapy is undertaken. I will attempt to identify some of the major causes of the disease afflicting the collective bargaining process and to suggest possible therapeutic actions.

It is not within the scope of this essay to examine all of the causes of the current illness afflicting collective bargaining. To a considerable degree, it stems from other problems of our society that only indirectly affect the process of bargaining. Such factors as racial tension and what has come to be called the "revolt against authority" have had detrimental effects on relations between management and the unions and on their relations with individual employees or union members. Therefore I will confine myself to two major sources of illness. The first is the use, or misuse, of power. The second is the political character of bargaining as we know it in this country.

The term "collective bargaining" is too often assumed to relate almost exclusively to the process by which contractual agreements are reached between management and unions. While the negotiation of agreements is an essential feature of bargaining, it is by no means the total process. At least equally important, and perhaps more important in the final analysis, is the art or technique of living with the results of negotiations. This phase of the process is not only the acid test of the negotiations that preceded it but is also likely to influence the outcome of future negotiations.

The excesses of power and politics take their toll, both during the negotiation of agreements and afterward. On the other hand, it may seem odd to consider power as a "problem," since power is what collective bargaining is all about. The primary historical purpose of union organization has been to enhance the power of employees vis-à-vis the employer. Why then consider power as one of the sources of collective bargaining's current illness? The reason is that when power becomes an end in itself it also becomes a force that can destroy any process of which it is a part. There is cause for concern that such a force exists already and constitutes a serious threat to collective bargaining.

The bargaining process contains four major sources of power, each of which deserves careful examination. One is the employer. Another is the union as an institution. The third comprises the union members, individually and collectively. The fourth is the government, whose primary role is to represent the "public interest."

The Employer as a Source of Power

The common stereotype of the employer as a giant corporation having many operations, employing thousands of people, and probably dealing with many different unions grossly misrepresents reality. The typical employer engaged in collective bargaining employs less than a thousand employees and supplies a limited group of services or products to a local or regional market. The financial resources available to his company are far from unlimited. That fact and the competitive nature of the marketplace are likely to cause him to place a rather high premium on continuity of operations.

It is unfortunate that so much of the publicity relating to collective bargaining usually concerns large corporations or groups of employers on the one hand and international unions on the other. The potential economic and social impact of strikes and settlements in such major negotiations understandably warrants more news attention than do negotiations and settlements on a smaller scale. Nevertheless, the vast majority of collective bargaining relationships *are* on a much smaller scale, although no less important from the standpoint of the parties directly involved.

Whatever the size or primary business of the employer, the nature of his power with respect to the collective bargaining situation is economic. He has the right, properly exercised, to decide to go out of business, either temporarily or permanently. That right normally constitutes his only significant source of bargaining power.

There was a time when many employers, or various groups representing them, had political power of a kind that might have affected labor-management relations. Such cases have become increasingly rare, however. Even the economic power of employers as a group has diminished significantly in recent decades. Among the major causes have been the following: (1) a closer balance between demand and the supply of labor; (2) an increasingly mobile labor force; (3) increased levels of general education; (4) growth of union power and political influence; (5) vastly expanded scope and power of government; (6) greatly increased communication of information throughout the country; and (7) increasing competition in world markets, including competition by imports in domestic markets.

Employers typically are less concerned about the fact of the erosion of their power than they are about the degree of that erosion. The concept of a balance of opposing forces is basic to our society and political system. William Green, then president of the American Federation of Labor, implicitly recognized this concept in his testimony before two congressional committees in 1935. He told the Senate Education and Labor Committee that "the economic conditions which exist today can be corrected only when the bargaining power of the employees is made equal to that of the employers." Before the House Committee on Labor, he noted that ". . . the fundamental necessity [is] for establishment of equality of bargaining power between employer and employee."[1]

The view of fair-minded employer groups today is that the pendulum has swung far beyond any reasonable definition of "equality." Their concern is well founded when it is realized that the scope of collective bargaining has been greatly expanded since World War II. It now includes areas

1 Sadler, Marion, "Who Speaks for the People in Collective Bargaining?" *Columbia Journal of World Business* 4 (March–April 1968): 21–26.

that relate to the direct management of the business, many of which can have a substantial effect on productive efficiency. Thus, the balance of power has been weighted to favor the unions at the same time that collective bargaining has reached into areas once reserved to management discretion. As one consequence, the collective bargaining process itself has been put in jeopardy. To work successfully, any process designed to resolve conflicts and differences of opinion must take place under conditions that make agreement possible. This requirement cannot be met in the absence of an approximate balance of power.

To summarize, the last thirty years have witnessed a sharp erosion of the economic power of the typical employer. That erosion has been accompanied by the virtual disappearance of whatever political power employers may once have been able to exert in their relations with labor. Meanwhile, a great expansion in the scope of collective bargaining has occurred. Each of these changes has tended to undermine the position of the employer in the bargaining process.

The Union as a Source of Power

A discussion of the nature and scope of union power should recognize the existence of at least three organizational levels of the labor movement: the federation, the international union, and the local union. The usual connotations of the term "union power" relate to the federation and the international union levels. The power of the local is primarily the power of its membership rather than of the union as an organizational entity. This aspect of union power will be discussed separately.

The power of the labor movement at the federation and international union levels is the single most important fact in contemporary collective bargaining. By any measure, that power is awesome. Its size is reflected not only in the pressure that can be brought to bear against an employer or group of employers but also in the potential effect that union actions can have on the general welfare and on the economy as a whole. A decision by one or a few union leaders to close down the ports or transportation system of most or all of the nation can send shock waves throughout the economy. It was reliably reported in 1968 that organized labor in New York ". . . was ready to immobilize the metropolis . . . in support of the garbage strikers. . . . Labor leaders bluntly told [public officials] that not a bus or subway train would roll, not a truck wheel would turn, and that the Utility Workers Union Local 1–2 was prepared to slash all electric power. There would have been no food, no fuel, no medicine, no nothing."[2]

Another facet of union power that has direct implications for collective bargaining is the immense financial resources of organized labor, combined with the willingness of labor leadership to use these resources to support political candidates and causes. This financial support probably deserves more credit for explaining the political power of unions than does the claim that the union leadership can "deliver the vote" to favored candidates.

The Labor-Management Relations Act of 1947 placed certain prohibitions on union expenditures in direct support

[2] Victor Riesel, "Inside Labor," column published by Hall Syndicate, New York, N.Y., September 24, 1968.

of candidates in federal elections. Loopholes in the law, however, have permitted unions to continue to give large amounts to candidates favored by the labor movement. It would be naïve to assume that the added political power thus generated does not significantly affect the collective bargaining process in this country.

The growth of union power in the last thirty years has been both cause and effect of the shift of labor's philosophy from the "bread and butter" bargaining aims of Samuel Gompers and William Green toward an increasingly active involvement in political and social causes and organizations. Within the collective bargaining arena itself, moreover, union organizations have typically set their sights on bargaining objectives that limit or even reduce productivity. The rationalizations usually presented in defense of these efforts sooner or later highlight the claim that automation breeds unemployment.[3] The blatant use of union power to curtail the productive efficiency of U.S. industry while at the same time inflating the direct cost of labor cannot be justified. Its impact is reflected in the fact that unit labor costs in U.S. manufacturing industries increased 10 percent in the twenty-four-month period ending August 1968. A continuation of this trend will be disastrous to the economic vitality of this country.

The power of most unions at the federation and international levels in this country far exceeds that needed to establish a reasonable equilibrium among the direct par-

[3] For a well-reasoned rebuttal of this claim, see Ralph W. Ellis, "Is Automation Causing Our High Unemployment?" *Personnel* (American Management Association), July–August 1963, pp. 8–17.

ticipants in the collective bargaining process. The remarks made by AFL-CIO President George Meany in opening the convention of the International Association of Machinists in September 1968 show that the leadership of the labor movement is well aware of the power at its disposal.[4]

Union Membership as a Source of Power

Whatever influence union membership is able to exert at higher organizational levels within the labor movement is exerted primarily through individual local unions. Union organizers take pains to stress that membership in a union can in itself be a source of power to the individual member. It may not only provide him with a certain degree of bargaining power in confronting his employer, but his membership may also permit him to obtain some degree of recognition and personal power within the local union hierarchy.

The power of local union membership tends to reach a peak shortly after the union is organized. One reason is that the decision by a majority of the group to form a local union must now be justified. In addition, the still recent promises made by those responsible for the organizational effort are freshly in mind. At least partial fulfillment of these promises is anticipated in return for the payments of dues and any applicable initiation fees. Furthermore, leadership within the local may not yet have begun to emerge,

[4] Meany is reported to have included the following statements in his remarks: " 'Some people, of course, say that we are doing too well, that we have too much power. . . . Well, if we have too much power, that's o.k. with me. Let's have some more of the same.' " Bureau of National Affairs, *Daily Labor Report,* September 9, 1968.

placing a premium on action by those who aspire to personal power or prominence within it. Whatever the causes, the early months following the organization of a local union tend to be marked by a heady feeling of power on the part of the membership. In time, various factors serve to bring about more stability and a greater sense of responsibility, a situation that is usually beneficial to the collective bargaining process. Thus it is generally in the interest both of the international union and of the employer for a local union to pass through the initial stages of power-consciousness rather quickly.

The process of stabilization typically occurs in the form of a gradual shift of power from the members themselves to their newly elected officials, and then through them to higher levels of the union organization. The rate at which this shift of power takes place depends on various factors, although it generally occurs more quickly and more completely than unions are prone to admit. In any case, the process is usually reversible at the will of the local membership. The power at the disposal of the membership which may be brought to bear on local union officials can be formidable. Given proper democratic procedures, it may be exercised in connection with the election or reelection of local officials, when ratification of a proposed new or changed agreement with the employer is recommended, or during the course of living under the existing agreement. The life of a local union official can indeed be a harried one if he lacks the support of at least a significant portion of the membership.

On the other hand, the power of the union membership

to bring pressure on union officials above the local level is sometimes exaggerated. The average lengthy tenure of international union officials testifies to this fact. Although there have been noteworthy cases where a change of international officials has occurred against the will of the incumbents, these cases have been widely noted partly because they have also been the exception that proves the rule. Moreover, the changes that have occurred among international union elected officials have been the result of power struggles among the union hierarchy at least as often as they have represented a grass-roots movement at the membership level.

It is difficult to take much comfort from some of the changes that are taking place or that are foreseeable with respect to union membership power. The emergence of a new generation of relatively well informed and articulate members portends a considerable reduction in the predictability of union behavior. This fact, plus the more general revolt against authority that appears to be taking place in our society, would be cause enough for concern. The increasing organization of professional and white-collar groups, particularly in the public sector, will also tend to generate an active and unpredictable exercise of power by union membership.

To survive as a vital institution in the years ahead, collective bargaining must prove able to adapt to the often substantial shifts of power that have occurred and will occur between union memberships on the one hand and their elected officials on the other. The potential consequences of these shifts are of real significance, both with respect to the process of reaching constructive agreements and with respect to the ability to live with those agreements during their effective term.

Government Power and Politics

Although this section will be concerned primarily with the impact of the federal government on collective bargaining, the importance of local and state governments in this regard should not be overlooked. These levels of government are more and more becoming massive employers in their own right, whose actions may well establish significant patterns or precedents in the collective bargaining area, as various unions proceed with the organization of their employees.

A key determinant of the future of collective bargaining in the United States will be our ability to resolve the issue of the right of public employees to strike. This complex issue has been of concern for many years. It has been said that the candidacy of Calvin Coolidge for President was strongly aided by the recollection of his statement during the Boston police strike in 1919 to the effect that "there is no right to strike against the public safety of anybody, anywhere, at any time." President Franklin D. Roosevelt took a similar position almost twenty years later in a letter to the National Federation of Federal Employees:

> All government employees should realize that the process of collective bargaining, as usually understood, cannot be transplanted into public service. Particularly, I want to emphasize my conviction that militant tactics have no place in the functions of any organization of government employees. . . . [A] strike of public employees manifests nothing less than an intent on their part to prevent or obstruct the operations of government until their demands are satisfied.

Such action, looking toward the paralysis of government by those who have sworn to support it, is unthinkable and intolerable.

The deterioration of collective bargaining can hardly be better illustrated than by comparing these statements with the situation confronting New York City in 1968 when it faced concurrent strike threats from policemen, firemen, teachers, sanitation workers, and certain electric utility workers. If an adequate solution to the problem of collective bargaining in the public sector cannot be found, all other efforts to avoid the demise of free collective bargaining may prove to be in vain.

State and local governments can have a second important effect on collective bargaining through the settlements that are reached in their contract negotiations, as well as through wage or benefit increases that may be determined unilaterally. Whether these increases are the result of negotiation or of legislative action, they can have a substantial influence on negotiated settlements in the private sector. They may not only establish a pattern for other settlements, but they may also influence the ability of government officials at the state and local level to serve effectively as mediators or conciliators in private disputes.

The third important influence on collective bargaining of government below the federal level relates to the exercise of police power. An impasse in bargaining frequently leads some union members to take a kind of action that poses at least a potential threat to the property or legal rights of the employer, other employees, or third parties. The willingness and ability of local government, and sometimes state government, to enforce the law with an even hand can be of major significance in the eventual resolution of individual collective bargaining situations.

If the powers of state and local governments tend to have an important influence on collective bargaining and its future, the same can be said with even greater emphasis with respect to the federal government. Among the major sources of the federal government's impact are the following: (1) legislation relating to the formation of unions and to the scope and process of collective bargaining; (2) the exercise of administrative and judicial power in areas directly or indirectly affecting the collective bargaining process; (3) conciliation, mediation, or direct intervention in disputes that have not been resolved by the parties themselves; (4) the government's own policies and actions as employer of a vast and expanding number of public employees; (5) direct or indirect effect on terms and conditions of employment through wage and hour regulations, administration of public contracts, resort to wage guidelines or direct wage controls, and regulation of benefit programs.

The enormously expanded role that government has come to play in collective bargaining is partly a reflection of the increase of government power and control on virtually all fronts in our society. That increase has probably been accentuated with regard to collective bargaining by the fact that retaining the goodwill and support of organized labor is assumed to have significant political advantages.

Some agencies of the federal govenrment seem to show less and less concern for the public interest in the collective bargaining area while at the same time actively fostering the growth of union power. Although this misadventure in government is not confined to the National Labor Relations Board, no department or agency has shown more bias in recent years. The propensity of the NLRB to "make law" instead of contenting itself with the administration of laws that have been passed by Congress is all too well known.

In testifying before the Senate Subcommittee on Separation of Powers in late 1968, a recognized authority on labor legislation and former regional attorney for the NLRB said that "while other administrative agencies generally have kept abreast of the socio-economic changes in the areas that are regulated, the NLRB persisted in its 1935 vision of employers and unions." An often-overlooked impact of NLRB policy and philosophy was brought into focus by the following testimony of Senator Robert P. Griffin, coauthor of the 1959 Landrum-Griffin Act:

> In the minds of some, any criticism of the NLRB is casually dismissed as just part of a power struggle going on between big business and big unions. Nothing could be further from the truth. More often, those who actually suffer from the distorted and twisted rulings of the Board are the individual workers, small unions, small businessmen, and the public at large.[5]

It is doubtful whether any factor has been more responsible for the current crisis in collective bargaining than has the misuse of government power, particularly at the federal level. Far too often, that vast power has been used to serve political ends rather than to nurture and maintain an effective process for minimizing and resolving disputes between

5 These quotations are from "Does NLRB Follow the Law?" *NAM Reports,* September 16, 1968, issued by the National Association of Manufacturers, Washington, D.C.

employers and unions, as well as for protecting the interest of individual employees and union members.

It is a matter of record (and what appears to be more than mere coincidence) that as the full force of decisions increasing union power has evolved, industrial strife has increased. . . . It is submitted that a major cause of growing labor strife and inflationary settlements against the public interest may be found by examining labor decisions as a point of departure.[6]

It is less important to attempt to assess the extent to which the powers of government may have contributed to the current illness of the collective bargaining process than it is to determine how these same powers can assist in the cure. As a start, government officials must learn to avoid acting in such a way as to worsen the existing illness. Government must also take into account its inevitable impact on the collective bargaining process, in the exercise of its authority as well as in its role as the largest single employer in our economy.

Treating the Illness

The discussion so far has pointed out that the imbalance of power and the political realities characteristic of collective bargaining are not the only causes for the present crisis but that they are two of the primary ones. Since they may reasonably be considered indigenous, we need to devise steps that might help to mitigate or offset them.

Well-intentioned corrective efforts may fall victim to two sources of error. The first is the tendency to deal with

[6] Harry L. Browne, "The Court, the NLRB and Free Collective Bargaining—A Second Look," *American Bar Association Journal* 54 (June 1968): 560–564.

symptoms rather than causes. In the case of collective bargaining, this is apparent in efforts that are concerned solely with minimizing strikes or providing economically sounder negotiation settlements. Even if such efforts achieved a measure of success, their effect would probably be short lived.

The second common source of error is the tendency to want to "pass a law" or press for some other form of government action. This route may well have to be considered as a last resort, but it is too often considered first. Attempts to deal with problems of collective bargaining by governmental edict are only likely to make the disease worse. There assuredly are some things that various levels of government can and should do if the collective bargaining crisis is to be solved, but it would be well to look first to some other steps that do not place the primary burden on the government.

Recognition by Unions and Employers of Their Respective Stakes No real solution to the collective bargaining crisis will be found unless the parties directly involved recognize the stake each of them has in making the process work satisfactorily. The likely alternatives that have so far been identified would probably prove much less desirable from the standpoint of either employers or unions than collective bargaining as we know it.

Whether or not to substitute an alternative for the present process may not be entirely discretionary with unions and employers. The choice is likely to be made for them if ways cannot be found to make the process and its consequences more compatible with the public interest than they have been in recent years. It is most assuredly in the self interest of both employers and unions to make collective bargaining work within and for the public interest.

Need for Effective Dialogue In order to make collective bargaining work, ways must be found to create a more effective dialogue concerning its problems. This dialogue must directly involve the parties themselves and not be limited to students or observers of the collective bargaining scene. It will require a degree of objectivity both on the part of unions and of employers, as well as of those speaking on their behalf, that has not been typical up to now. Instead, we have seen self-serving propaganda designed to win the support of public opinion for one position or another.

An effective dialogue does not require that the parties publicly agree with one another's point of view. They must be prepared, however, for a thoughtful exchange of views without crying "Foul!" each time the other makes a valid point. The all-too-frequent distortions and misrepresentations of the collective bargaining process, either in specific cases or in general, must be avoided. Members of the academic community who are knowledgeable about collective bargaining can play an effective role in bringing about constructive dialogue, by helping the parties to learn to deal with facts and also to substitute reasonable, calm judgment for fear and histrionics.

One promising effort to develop a better understanding among employers and unions was the formation in early 1968 of the Institute of Collective Bargaining and Group Relations. The Institute is said to have two prime objectives: ". . . to improve the process of collective bargaining internally, and to give the public a better understanding of how it works and why it is important in a democratic society."[7] It is to be hoped that the work of the institute will contribute to the dialogue needed to strengthen collective bargaining.

Union Members Must Develop a Broader Perspective The bargaining process is unlikely to survive in recognizable form unless some method is found to provide union members with a broader perspective than the simple aim to "get it while the getting's good." More than a few union members already recognize that such an objective is self-defeating. Many others would do so if they were not being regularly encouraged in the opposite direction by union officials, political candidates, and others. What is needed is an intensive and constructive educational process in which employers, unions, and government would have to join to achieve success.

The great majority of American employees are fully capable of understanding that it is not in the long-range interest of either the country or the labor force to have labor costs consistently rising faster than productivity. Relatively few employees understand this today. There is an urgent need for a conscious and deliberate effort to undo some of the common misunderstandings that exist regarding basic economic facts of life. If the need is not met, one consequence is likely to be that collective bargaining will be replaced by one of its less desirable alternatives.

Unions and Employers Must Learn to Deal with the "Generation Gap" One of the most significant threats to respon-

7 Theodore Kheel, "A Collective Bargaining Institute," *American Labor* 1 (July 1968): 17–21.

sible, self-disciplined union policy and practice is the phenomenon of the so-called "generation gap." The extent of this gap is a relatively recent fact of life, both for unions and for our society as a whole. It is a significant problem in many union organizations and is likely to continue to have a real impact on collective bargaining for some time to come. Many unions are experiencing an influx of younger members who are somewhat better educated and who have been raised in a different social and political environment than that of their parents and older fellow union members. Many in this younger group are not willing to settle for traditional approaches to union affairs and administration, although they might have proved successful in the past.

This phenomenon has many implications for both employers and unions. From the standpoint of collective bargaining, it constitutes a significant source of instability. It will continue to do so until appropriate adjustments are made both by unions and by employers. There is reason to believe that at least some employers have been more responsive to this relatively new development than has been typical of union officials. One analysis has pointed out that

continuation of the institutional approach to collective bargaining to the virtual exclusion of developments in the behavioral sciences, particularly those pertaining to management theory and practice, could conceivably effect a sizable reduction in union bargaining power and influence within business organizations. Unions (and others) must begin to take notice of the shift in management thought brought about by behavioral scientists if they are to avoid compounding the crisis in collective bargaining.[8]

Much remains to be learned about how the generation gap

[8] Arthur A. Thompson and Irwin Weinstock, "Facing the Crisis in Collective Bargaining," *MSU Business Topics* 16 (Summer 1968): 37.

affects collective bargaining. It is not clear that either unions or employers have made measurable progress in attempting to adjust to it. The current illness afflicting collective bargaining makes it highly desirable that some effective solutions be found with respect to this source of instability.

Changes in Government Policy and Practice The role of government as legislator, administrator, and direct employer is so critical to the collective bargaining process that no conceivable solutions have a chance of achieving a cure in the absence of certain changes that can occur only with the direct participation of government. To begin with, government policy and action must face squarely the serious disequilibrium of bargaining power that presently exists. The imbalance is not limited solely to unions as opposed to private employers but also applies in an alarming degree to the clearly demonstrated power of unions when they confront the government as a direct employer.

The present disequilibrium gives a substantial and sometimes harmful advantage to many unions. It does so at the expense of consumers, employers, many individual union members, and the unorganized majority of the labor force. A continuation of the present trend is very likely to have critical effects on our society, our domestic economy, and the U.S. position in world markets.

A thorough analysis of all of the major changes needed in government policy and practice to bring about a cure for the current disease from which collective bargaining is suffering would require much more lengthy treatment than is appropriate here. Some of the major directions can be identified, however.

Much attention has been given to the desirability of applying the traditional antitrust policy of the federal government to unions. It is by no means certain that antitrust policy has been either effective or beneficial with respect to organizations to which it has been applied to date. It is even less certain that it would provide an effective means of dealing with union power.

A much more promising approach would be to undertake a careful and objective review of current laws that relate to collective bargaining. As has already been pointed out here and elsewhere, much of the current federal law and procedure in this area date from a time when the basic situation was very different. Consequently, they are addressed to needs and circumstances that are not consistent with present realities.

Even more urgent than a review and overhauling of legislation pertaining to collective bargaining is the need for more evenhanded administration of the laws that do exist. The political nature of government must be subordinated to its judicial responsibilities in this highly sensitive area if collective bargaining is to be nurtured and strengthened rather than stifled and eventually suffocated. To attempt to exhort or compel restraint in collective bargaining settlements at the same time that little, if any, restraint is being shown in granting wage increases to government employees is an exercise in futility. For government to represent itself as an objective monitor of union representation issues in private industry while at the same time inviting and encouraging organization of public employees is not likely to inspire total confidence.

In short, government at all levels needs to rethink its impact on collective bargaining. It is to be hoped that this rethinking will provide greater objectivity and some new directions, both with respect to legislation and to the exercise of administrative and judicial responsibility.

Conclusion

It has been the thesis of this essay that (1) collective bargaining is seriously ill, (2) that the sickness need not be fatal, but that (3) it is likely to be so if effective and timely therapy is not applied. It is essential that the parties directly involved in the collective bargaining process accept the prime responsibility for bringing about a cure. If they are to be successful, the efforts of employers and unions must be complemented by the firm support of all levels of government.

7
Reflections on a Generation of Work in the Field of Labor Economics

John G. Turnbull

This essay comments on the changing character of labor economics as a field of study over the last thirty years, the professional generation of Douglass Brown.

The Role of Labor in Economics

Perhaps the single most outstanding change that has taken place, and the most obvious one, is that labor economics is not the fashionable specialty it once was. From outside the discipline, two forces have been at work. First, the "problems" that stimulated student interest in the field have been attacked and substantially resolved.[1] The right to organize and bargain collectively is an accomplished fact, much social legislation has been enacted, and many of the severe "economic" problems experienced by working people in the 1930s have disappeared. Second, other economic problems, like economic development, are at the center of interest. There has been a push-pull effect; students have been pulled into fields of growing importance and interest, and they have been pushed out of labor by the relative decrease in the importance of "labor problems."

[1] Except for the "grape boycott" issue of 1968, this writer has seen little of the kind of emotional involvement that existed among students of labor in the 1930s. And student involvement in the 1968 grape boycott appears—at least at this writer's institution—to have been strongest among those who have never had a course in labor (let alone economics).

Inside the field of economics, other forces have had their effect. Institutional economics, the intellectual domain of most of the labor economists, has given away to theoretical analysis. It is now rare to find an economist who is not trained in mathematics and some statistics. A generation ago, a labor specialist who had substantial training in mathematics was a rarity. If a contemporary economist addresses policy questions, and many do, he is unlikely to find the labor problems analytically challenging. On the sociometric scale of economics these days, labor ranks low.

The consequences of these changes are not hard to discern. At the undergraduate level, labor courses do not draw the enrollments they once did. The introductory courses may hold up well, but in advanced subjects interest slackens perceptibly. At the graduate level, fewer students choose labor as their specialty, and those who do seem to lack the talent for analysis of students specializing in mathematical economics or econometrics. At the University of Minnesota, a "labor" Ph.D. appears approximately once every two years, whereas in other specialties the output is much higher. At the postdoctoral or faculty level, labor economists are productive, yet many of the significant contributions to the field of labor over the last decade or two have been the result of work by nonlabor specialists.

None of these observations should be taken either as a lament for the current state of affairs or as a plea for a rekindled interest. Other problems have appeared in the real world and in the intellectual domain, and the response has been exactly what one would expect in the free market of ideas.

The Changing Character of Labor as a Subject in the Economics Curriculum

As the field of labor was broadly defined a generation ago, it included courses in personnel administration and labor relations (though they may not have been technically listed as economics subjects). The number of such courses, however, tended to be few, they were general in nature, and not infrequently they had an antiunion orientation. Today the picture is very different. At the University of Minnesota, for example, 36 courses are offered in personnel administration and labor relations compared with 6 a quarter century ago. By way of contrast, the university offers a total of 6 labor economics courses.

Many industrial relations courses are highly specialized and no longer tend to have any inherent antiunion bias. These courses are taught in schools of business administration and colleges of commerce as they were a generation ago. Enrollments have increased markedly. Individuals who a generation ago might have specialized in labor economics have turned largely to the industrial relations specialty. This shift is particularly true of foreign students. The institutional content of labor economics in areas such as public policy and economic security tends to be oriented to the policies and practices of the United States. Hence, much of it is "nontransferable" from the standpoint of the foreign student.

Much of the training in industrial relations, on the other hand, is transferable. Understanding of manpower management practices—recruitment, selection, training, promotion, downgrading, layoff, wage and salary administration, and so on—can be applied in other economies the world over. At Minnesota there are two or three Ph.D. candidates in industrial relations every year and over a dozen M.A. candidates. In labor economics there are no M.A. candidates and, as noted earlier, only one Ph.D. candidate every two years.[2] Again there is a push-pull effect. Students are pulled into a field in which demand has greatly increased, particularly for practitioners; they (particularly students from other countries) are pushed out of subject areas in which the content is largely nontransferable.

That in the field of labor economics itself there are forces that are shrinking its scope is especially evident in the area of public policy, where the vast array and complexity of legislation has shifted the emphasis away from the economist to the lawyer. Some basic economic content, of course, has survived: the nature of labor markets and their regulation, the strike as a shutting off of supply, the boycott as a sealing off of demand. But much has passed to the legal specialist: contract bars, the captive audience doctrine, runoff elections, and other issues that are without economic relevance. It is no accident that a best-selling text in the field is by a lawyer, not an economist.[3] Much the same is true of labor history. In many institutions it is in the province of history departments. Economic security has be-

[2] An M.A. in industrial relations was introduced at Minnesota in 1955, and 158 M.A. degrees were awarded up to mid-1968. A number of these graduates are already vice-presidents for "industrial relations" in large companies.

[3] C. O. Gregory, *Labor and the Law*, 2nd rev. ed., with 1961 supplement (New York: W. W. Norton, 1961). It should be noted, however, that there is much sophisticated economics in this volume.

come so interrelated with the field of insurance that it is increasingly taught in schools of business administration.

The changing, and increasingly detailed, content of labor courses, especially in the field of public policy, has created great difficulties for the teacher. What, logically, is the scope and content of a course in public policy? Where does one stop at presenting the "facts" with respect to labor legislation? I have run several polarized experiments in recent years on the content of my public policy course. In one instance, during a summer session (approximately 22 fifty-minute class periods), I used a very general approach to the subject.[4] In another, an evening-school class (approximately the equivalent of 25 fifty-minute periods), the Labor Management Relations Act itself was the text, and some 20 periods focused upon Section 8 of the act. Neither version was particularly successful. In the former, students felt they gained a better understanding of the general dimensions of public policy, but the course did not meet a manifest desire for information about election procedures, recognition picketing, hot-cargo clauses, and so on. In the latter version, the students who were working practitioners were satisfied,[5] but the liberal arts and general education students characterized the course as "intellectual garbage."

It is possible, of course, to travel a middle road. And it is possible to give a public policy course a high economic content—to give it in an economic framework. But the

4 The text was Robert Evans, Jr., *Public Policy toward Labor* (New York: Harper & Row, 1965).

5 I was careful to point out, however, that I was not a legal specialist and that in the event of a real-world problem competent counsel should be sought.

problem still remains: what should be the content of a meaningful course in public policy for the liberal arts student? Perhaps there is no answer (if any reader has one, I should like to hear about it), and the problem will arise every time the course is restructured.[6]

This same problem obtains at the graduate level. At Minnesota we do not expect a Ph.D. candidate in labor economics to be prepared for written examinations in collective bargaining, economic security, labor history, public policy, union organization, and administration. "Institutional" options have been provided to supplement the basic core of labor "theory" required of all students. To expect familiarity with the details of all major legislation is patent nonsense.[7]

In summary, what one finds is: (1) A lesser rank for "labor problems," compared to a generation ago. (2) The passing of institutional economics with an accompanying change in subject matter and training within economics. This has had the effect of shifting the place of labor in the discipline.

[6] In many specialties, this problem does not seem to arise. In public finance, for example, tax law does not receive nearly the detailed attention that labor law does in a public policy course. In money and banking courses there is institutional content, but it is small compared to labor courses. In international trade one does not memorize the details of the Kennedy Round tariffs. There is much theoretical content in these specialties upon which the courses can be built. We do not have a "theory" of public policy in labor, or if we do I am unaware of it. Hence the need for detail. Government regulation of business comes closest to labor in that it requires knowledge of the Sherman, Clayton, and other acts, but such courses have a considerable body of underlying theory.

[7] There is a story (apocryphal?) that at another institution, more analytically oriented, a Ph.D. candidate in labor had never heard of the Taft-Hartley Act.

(3) A marked development of "industrial relations"—personnel administration and labor relations—which has attracted many students who a generation ago might have gravitated to labor economics. (4) The increasingly technical nature of much of the institutional content of the "labor" field, which has made the subject more appropriate for law schools, history departments, and insurance specialties in schools of business administration.

None of this should be taken as a cry of sorrow for labor economics. Although the scene has shifted, there is still much basic economic content in the labor area, and there is much solid research. This research, however, is being carried out by economists with sophisticated training who are not, strictly speaking, labor economists. The most thoroughgoing inquiry into the impact of unionism upon wages has been conducted by an economist who could hardly be classified as an institutionalist, or even as basically as a "labor" economist.[8] The situation is the same in other research areas: Phillips curve analysis, incomes policies, guaranteed minimum incomes, the negative income tax, and so on.[9]

Changes in Educational Institutional Structures and in Educational Training

Labor economics is now but one subject in the more comprehensive field of manpower. How did this come about? In the period 1935–1945, the view emerged that labor eco-

[8] H. Gregg Lewis, *Unionism and Relative Wages in the United States: An Empirical Inquiry* (Chicago: University of Chicago Press, 1963).

[9] For example, two of the major contributions on the negative income tax are by Milton Friedman and James Tobin.

nomics was not the proper framework for the study of man in the context of work. This shift was accompanied by a variety of structural changes. Schools, centers, and departments of industrial relations, personnel administration, and labor relations were established. Before World War II there were only four formally structured industrial relations centers in educational institutions: at Princeton, M.I.T., Michigan, and Stanford. Today there are fifty to sixty.

These entities serve varying purposes. The "school" of industrial relations is the most comprehensive and combines teaching, degree granting, research, and public service. The New York State School of Labor and Industrial Relations is, perhaps, the outstanding example. "Centers," for the most part, are research-oriented. "Departments" are primarily degree-oriented units to which the student is attached in the course of his study.

What type of training does the field of industrial relations afford? I was an early recipient of such training (though technically my degree was in economics), and the comments that follow are based on my personal experience. The main characteristic of industrial relations training is its eclecticism, a source both of strength and of weakness. A major advantage is the broad exposure to manpower problems from a variety of viewpoints, rather than from the perspective of economics alone. Such training, however, does not produce a specialist, unless one defines industrial relations itself as a specialty. One can teach introductory courses in labor economics, in personnel administration and labor relations, and advanced work in collective bargaining and public policy, but one lacks the specialized knowledge of the psychologist, the lawyer, and the economist which is required for much of the subject matter. The industrial relations teacher is likely to know a little about a lot of things but may be a man without a country.

Whether or not industrial relations should be viewed as a discipline, it has its own organizations (for example, the Industrial Relations Research Association), its own meetings, its own journals (for example, the *Industrial and Labor Relations Review*), and, in a general sense, its own "culture." True, there is interaction with other groups, as in joint programming at annual meetings with, say, the American Economics Association. But increasingly it has acquired a real and separate identity,[10] a process that is likely to continue in the future.

I have concluded that for an undergraduate and for the M.A. candidate who intends to become a practitioner, training in industrial relations is a useful education. For the Ph.D. student, however, the study of economics, with a good background in theory and qualitative methods (or in psychology with its specialized training areas), is to be preferred. This conclusion holds even more if one wishes to undertake research. (I would suggest again that many if not most of the recent important research results in labor have

10 Of the 69 presidents of the American Economics Association, 7 could be regarded as having had some labor specialization: John R. Commons, Jacob H. Hollander, George E. Barnett, Harry A. Millis, Sumner H. Slichter, Paul H. Douglas, and Edwin E. Witte. With the possible exception of Douglas and Slichter, all these men could be regarded as institutionalists. Parenthetically, I would hazard the guess that it will be a long time before another labor specialist ascends to the presidency of the association.

been contributed by the specialist, though one can produce certain examples to the contrary.)[11]

In summary, one now finds the following structure: (1) Increasing numbers of industrial relations units, with identifiable industrial relations curricula, have been set up in educational institutions. (2) These units are serviced in a variety of ways, in some cases by specialists from disciplinary departments. (3) The units tend to become self-contained. As they become more self-contained, they hire their own specialists, such as economists and psychologists. It is my belief that such specialists are not as able as their colleagues in departments of economics or psychology. As industrial relations becomes a separate discipline, these units will tend to become "departments" in the conventional sense of the term. It will be interesting to see if industrial relations units acquire some new organizational form, or if they merely duplicate existing forms.

Research

Four factors characterize the change in research in the field of labor over the past generation:

1. A notable increase in the amount of research undertaken and in the published results. If one includes the related fields of personnel administration and labor relations, the increase is even more striking.[12]

[11] Some of my colleagues have taken issue with this statement. It would probably be more accurate to suggest that this appears more and more to be the case.

[12] I changed offices several years ago and found I had twenty-seven file boxes (*not* filing cases) of reprints dating back to 1945. The proliferation of labor journals has, of course, provided a much larger outlet

2. The sizable increase in "institutional" or "group" research, much of which is attributable to the growth of industrial relations centers. The large number of personnel at such centers today provides the critical mass necessary for organized research. Institutional ("institutional" is used here in a different sense) research has permitted problems to be tackled on a scale not dreamed of in decades past.

3. The subject matter of research and the approaches used have altered markedly. Earlier research was often of the "case study" kind, focusing on, for example, specific unions; much of it was related to labor and social legislation. That more recent research has tackled problems of a much different nature can be shown by several examples. The early post–World War II work on labor markets and labor mobility, sponsored by the Social Science Research Council, is a case in point. The massive studies of labor and management in developing economies undertaken by Dunlop, Harbison, Kerr, and Myers provide another illustration. Research has also become more sophisticated in its techniques. Although most labor economists even today are not highly trained as mathematicians or statisticians, quantitative analysis is common.

4. "Interdisciplinary" research, which became fashionable after World War II, has in my opinion been unsuccessful. The view of manpower problems as embracing economic, legal, psychological, and sociological dimensions has not

than existed a quarter century ago. Considering that labor is not the fashionable field it once was, it is amazing how much work is turned out! The current interest in "human resources" doubtless accounts for some of this output.

yielded a comprehensive new synthesis. Instead, interdisciplinary research seems to have produced results that simply add the view of the economist to that of the psychologist, the sociologist, and so on. The contributions of the late Douglas McGregor, another M.I.T. colleague, to our understanding of manpower are an exception, but there are few other examples wherein the interdisciplinary technique fulfilled its promise.

Some Conclusions and a Look at the Future

Douglass V. Brown received a Ph.D. in economics at Harvard in 1932 and has spent much of the last thirty-odd years in teaching and research in collective bargaining and public policy. It is doubtful that a generation from now we will find a Harvard Ph.D. in economics similarly engaged. The labor economist qua labor economist, a generation from now, will be sophisticated in the use of quantitative techniques, will be concerned with the "economics" of labor, and will be less concerned with institutional detail despite the high degree of such detail in the labor field. Much important work in the economics of labor will be done by nonlabor specialists in the areas of wage theory, incomes policies, collective bargaining, and inflation.

The labor curriculum in the economics department will be further truncated (and may disappear altogether). Outside of the introductory course, one will find a course in wages and wage theory, and, perhaps, one in collective bargaining.

Industrial relations will continue to grow and will be the main repository of labor topics. The student who wishes to specialize in manpower will be much more likely to receive his training through this route. Although there is nothing illogical about this, one is dismayed at the relative economic ignorance of many who choose this path.

If a discipline of industrial relations develops, it must cope with a complex and catholic mass of subject matter. Those who receive advanced degrees in economics will gravitate toward academic positions; industrial relations students, particularly at the M.A. level, will become practitioners. The school of business administration, or some unit other than the economics department, will be the organizational home of most labor subjects.

It is probably not wise even to question the "goodness" or "badness" of the changes in the field of labor studies in the last generation. In the time since Douglass V. Brown first came to M.I.T. in 1938, no other area of economics has undergone comparable change. The retirement of Professor Brown may coincide with the end of a chapter in the field to which he gave so much.

Index